9 95
15

245

Twayne's United States Authors Series

EDITOR OF THIS VOLUME

Warren French

Indiana University

Gwendolyn Brooks

TUSAS 395

Gwendolyn Brooks

GWENDOLYN BROOKS

By HARRY B. SHAW
University of Florida

TWAYNE PUBLISHERS
A DIVISION OF G. K. HALL & CO., BOSTON

Library of Congress Cataloging in Publication Data

Shaw, Harry B.   1937–
    Gwendolyn Brooks.

    (Twayne's United States authors series ; TUSAS 395)
    A revision of the author's thesis, University of
Illinois at Urbana-Champaign, 1972 which had title:
Social themes in the poetry of Gwendolyn Brooks.
    Bibliography: p. 189–96
    Includes index.
    1.   Brooks, Gwendolyn, 1917–   —Criticism and
interpretation.
PS3503.R7244Z88   1980   811'.54   80–24738
ISBN 0–8057–7287–1

Contents

About the Author

Harry B. Shaw was born in Union, Missouri, in 1937, the fourth of six children of Robert and Ethel Shaw. His father was a brickyard laborer and his mother taught school in Missouri and Illinois. When he was nine, his family moved to Edwardsville, Illinois, where he grew up attending the local elementary and high school.

In 1955 Shaw entered Illinois State University, majoring in English and minoring in speech. Upon graduation in 1959, he went to Chicago to teach English in the public schools. The following year he married Christiana Scott, a native of Edwardsville whom he had known since childhood.

It was while living on Chicago's South Side that Shaw became keenly aware of so many of the scenes depicted in Miss Brooks's poetry. At this time Gwendolyn Brooks had the reputation of being out of touch with the problems of blacks. But Shaw believes that there was always controlled protest in her poetry, especially in poems like "We Real Cool."

In 1964 Shaw returned to Illinois State University and received a master's degree in English, becoming an Instructor of English at Illinois State in 1965.

In 1967 Shaw moved to Champaign-Urbana, Illinois, to enroll in the doctoral program at the University of Illinois studying American and Afro-American literature. Here he met Drs. Keneth Kinnamon and Richard Barksdale, who helped to shape his interests and progress. Dr. Kinnamon helped him select and organize the topic for his dissertation, *Social Themes in the Poetry of Gwendolyn Brooks* (1972), out of which the present work has grown.

He received his Ph.D. in English in 1972 and in 1973 he was employed by the University of Florida in Gainesville, where he presently works as associate dean of the College of Liberal Arts and Sciences and as associate professor of English.

His research interests are in Afro-American literature with articles on imagery in Gwendolyn Brooks's poetry and trends in Afro-American literature and in popular culture.

Preface

While critical essays on even limited aspects of the poetry of Gwendolyn Brooks are still comparatively few in number for a poet of her accomplishments, no serious comprehensive analysis of her poetry as a whole has been published. Hence this book. Much of the writing on Miss Brooks's poetry consists of general reviews of single poems or of books of poetry. Miss Brooks has had five major books of poetry published (*A Street in Bronzeville, Annie Allen, The Bean Eaters, Selected Poems,* and *In the Mecca*) as well as several small books (*Riot, Family Pictures, Bronzeville Boys and Girls, The Tiger Who Wore White Gloves,* and *Beckonings*). Her lone novel is *Maud Martha.* Recognized by the literary establishment as a first-rate poet, she has won numerous awards and honors including the coveted Pulitzer Prize for Poetry in 1950 for *Annie Allen.* Other awards include the *Mademoiselle* Merit Award in 1945; the American Academy of Letters Award in 1946; a Guggenheim Fellowship in 1949; and the Friends of Literary Award for Poetry in 1964. She has also been named Poet Laureate of the State of Illinois and has been awarded honorary doctorates from Columbia College in Chicago, Lake Forest College, Elmhurst College, the Illinois Institute of Technology, Mundelein College, Skidmore College, Lewis College, Loyola University, Southern Illinois University, the University of Wisconsin, Northwestern University, Millikin University, Western Illinois University, De Paul University, and others.

The poetry of Gwendolyn Brooks has exemplified her poetic premise "to vivify the universal fact." Through her own microcosmic "postage stamp" of Chicago's South Side, she, like Faulkner with his Yoknapatawpha microcosm, achieves artistic excellence not by attempting to rise above the condition of the black ghetto but by raising the level where that condition is usually perceived. Thus presented, this condition becomes an aid to understanding man, enlightening readers through vivid vignettes of the black experience. An in-depth analysis of her poetry and novel will enhance understanding and appreciation of them as positive social forces.

The chief purpose of this study is to analyze the poetry and the prose of Gwendolyn Brooks in terms of the social themes that run through them: death, the fall from glory, the labyrinth, and survival. By taking note of the parallels between the vignettes depicted in Miss Brooks's works and various aspects of black life, the analysis will show that the themes expressed constitute a mimesis of black life and are rooted in the psychological and social realities of the black experience. The various social themes of death, the fall from glory, the labyrinth, and survival represent different but interrelated stages of development in the story of the experience of the black man of the United States. The order in which the themes are discussed in this study will follow the rough order in which they are introduced and emphasized in the total body of Miss Brooks's poetry. After Chapter 1 provides insight on her career and life and Chapter 2 gives a brief overview of her poetic approach and significance, the next chapters show how she realizes the aforementioned themes in individual poems. While the themes are for the most part conterminous entities, there is a certain logic to the order in which they appear. Chapter 3 depicts the most prevalent social reality of the black man's present state as spiritual death. Chapter 4 shows that it is from the vantage point of death that the black man views his former glory and freedom, the loss of which constitutes his spiritual death. Beyond the many indications of the mere existence of death, Chapter 5 focuses on the black man's effort to escape his peculiar kind of hell in the United States—groveling confusion of the labyrinth. In Chapter 6 the theme of survival with its components of restraint, militance, and rebirth offers an answer to death by envisioning the black man's enduring to solve the labyrinth and reclaim former glory. Finally, Chapter 7 examines the various themes in Miss Brooks's only novel, *Maud Martha*.

Covering the major themes of Miss Brooks's poetry, the chapters depict also major phases of the black American perspective. Drawn from the black experience, the vignettes of the poetry reveal the variety, complexity, and resilience of the black vista.

HARRY B. SHAW

University of Florida

Acknowledgments

For early encouragement and guidance on my doctoral dissertation, out of which this study grew, I am especially indebted to Dr. Keneth Kinnamon and to Dr. Richard Bardsdale, professors of English at the University of Illinois. Dr. Kinnamon also has been most helpful and supportive during the writing of this book. I extend particular appreciation to Miss Brooks, who patiently submitted to interviews and gave freely of her time and suggestions.

For the time spent with Henry Blakely, Val Gray Ward, George Kent, and Nora Blakely and for the insight gained from them about Miss Brooks's life and works I am deeply appreciative.

I am also grateful to my colleagues, friends, and family who have encouraged and inspired me, especially my wife, Christiana, who shares my warm regard for Miss Brooks and her work.

I am also indebted to my professional colleagues at the University of Florida, Drs. Bob Burton Brown, Harry Grater, Ward Hellstrom, Richard Green, and Ronald Foreman, for their encouragement, advice, patience, and willingness to alter their plans to accommodate my efforts.

For permission to quote from copyrighted material, acknowledgment is made to the following: Harper and Row, Publishers, for poems from *The World of Gwendolyn Brooks* (1971) and *Selected Poems* (1963); Broadside Press for poems and other materials from *Riot* (1969), *Family Pictures* (1970), *Beckonings* 1975), and *Report from Part One* (1972).

Chronology

1917   Gwendolyn Brooks born, June 7, in Topeka, Kansas, the first child of David and Keziah Brooks.
1917   Family moved to Chicago.
1933   Met James Weldon Johnson and Langston Hughes.
1934   Graduated from Englewood High School.
1936   Graduated from Wilson Junior College.
1939   Married Henry Blakely.
1940   Son, Henry, Jr., born on October 10.
1941   Attends Inez Stark class.
1943   Won Midwestern Writers' Conference poetry award in Chicago, Illinois.
1945   *A Street in Bronzeville;* Midwestern Writers' Conference at Northwestern University.
1948   Began to write reviews for Chicago newspapers.
1949   *Annie Allen.*
1950   Pulitzer Prize for *Annie Allen;* met Mary McCleod Bethune.
1951   Daughter, Nora, born on September 8.
1953   *Maud Martha* (novel).
1959   Father, David Brooks, died.
1960   *Bean Eaters.*
1963   *Selected Poems*; first teaching job at Chicago's Columbia College.
1964   Received from Columbia College her first honorary doctorate, Doctor in Humane Letters.
1967   Fisk University Black Writers' Conference; full-time duties at Chicago Teachers College, North.
1968   *In The Mecca*; Poet Laureate of Illinois.
1969   "Most stirring tribute," to Miss Brooks by black artists of Chicago; *Riot*; separated from husband in December.
1970   *Family Pictures*; Gwendolyn Brooks Black Cultural Center named for her at Western Illinois University.
1971   Small heart attack on Christmas Day forced her to give up

teaching; *The World of Gwendolyn Brooks*; switched to Broadside Press; *To Gwen with Love* published by admirers; trip to East Africa.

1972 *Report from Part One* (autobiography).

1974 Ended separation from husband, Henry Blakely.

1975 *Beckonings.*

1976 Brother, Raymond Brooks, died.

1978 Mother, Keziah Brooks, died.

CHAPTER 1

The Artist and the Person

I The Most Stirring Tribute

O N December 28, 1969, at the Afro-Arts Theater on Chicago's
South Side, Gwendolyn Brooks received what she considers
the most stirring and significant tribute of her life. It came from
many young black artists of Chicago—musicians, painters, poets,
dancers, and others who gathered in an exuberant festival filled
with rich color and music to pay public tribute to Gwendolyn
Brooks for her accomplishments as a poet and for her contribution to life in the black community. In her autobiography, *Report
from Part One*, Miss Brooks gives the following account of the
event:

> The most stirring tribute of my life, the most significant, was the
> extraordinary one created for me by Val Gray Ward, "our own"
> actress—her performing group, Kuumba, and many other young black
> artists of Chicago—on December 28 of 1969 at the Afro-Arts Theater.
> . . . And on my night, as on other rich occasions, we had Phil
> Cohran and his Artistic Heritage Ensemble, making black music, sure
> and strong and passionate, in the big barny place . . . Darlene and
> her dancers, hot flesh-wire across the stage . . . the poets, giving
> freely of themselves to the huge crowd they know wanted their
> product . . . the Kuumba players . . . The Pharoahs . . . the Mal-
> colmn X Community College Chorus . . . black stars! Lerone Ben-
> nett, Don L. Lee, Walter Bradford, Dudley Randall, Margaret Danner
> and Margaret Burroughs, Eugene Perkins, Sonia Sanchez, Sigmonde
> Wimberli, Carolyn Rodgers, Ronda Davis, Cynthia Conley (Zubena),
> Maxine Elliston, Johari; black painters with their portraits of myself,
> Jeff Donaldson, now chairman of Howard University's art depart-
> ment, Jon Lockard, Edward Christmas (who painted me into The Wall
> of Respect). . . . And—the Blackstone Rangers came, in force!—with
> tokens of affection, earnest personal congratulations.
> Costumes—art—release and joy. (*R*, 197)[1]

At the event Miss Brooks was happy knowing that she had so inspired and pleased this vibrant young group of artists whom she in turn admired so much. The festivities reflected the respect and love that she generated from the people like those who make up the characters in her poetic vignettes. *To Gwen with Love*, a tribute in book form that poured forth from this same group of artists and others, consists of many poems and other written exaltations of the virtues of Gwendolyn Brooks as a poet, a woman, a black person. Indeed, the festival tribute signaled a new queenhood for Miss Brooks among black artists and black people in general.

Befitting the queenhood bestowed on her and bespeaking subtly and effectively her devotion to and identification with the lives of black Americans, Miss Brooks names this event as the pinnacle of her literary acclaim—even above receiving the prestigious Pulitzer Prize which she had been awarded in 1950, the Poet Laureateship of Illinois which she received in 1968, and the many other literary honors she has received throughout her career. Miss Brooks, though very pleased, wondered at her seemingly sudden popularity and prestige. The explanations for this profound mutual admiration between poet and subject matter and for the surprise at her new queenhood are found partly in the black experience and partly in the personal experiences of her early childhood, school days, family life, marriage, motherhood, and writing career.

II   *Kansas Roots*

Miss Brooks's parents, Keziah Corine Wims and David Anderson Brooks, both native Kansans, provided a home full of love and encouragement for Gwendolyn and her brother, Raymond. Her father, a man she characterizes as "kind" and as having "rich artistic abilities" was born in Atchison, Kansas. He finished high school in Oklahoma City and attended Fisk University for one year, planning to become a doctor. These plans were aborted, however, when David moved to Chicago, where work conflicted with his medical training. In 1914 he met Keziah Wims, a native of Topeka, Kansas, and married her two years later.

The commonplace incidents which Gwendolyn Brooks remembers about her father are in themselves somewhat indicative of the love they shared and the mellow influence he had on her character and poetry. Whatever he did—whether reading stories, singing, giving recitations, or just smiling with his kind eyes— Gwendolyn and Raymond saw him as a figure of power. He was a super mechanic, thought surely able to fix anything. He could make a lasting fire in the furnace; he could chuckle in such a way that made him appear strong and secure. That Gwendolyn noticed these common traits and took inspiration from them reflects her propensity for being stimulated by and ascribing considerable significance to incidents and situations of everyday life.

Perhaps her father's stories about her paternal grandfather, Lucas Brooks, and his exploits as a runaway slave and later as head of his family helped to foster a sense of identity with the historical suffering among the poor and the destitute. She was told about Lucas marrying her grandmother Elizabeth and having twelve children and several of the children dying young. She was told also about evil landlords—one driving Lucas and his family away at gunpoint—and about her grandfather's mules being poisoned by those envious of him. She learned that Lucas, while operating a rooming house, was openly generous to beggars though living in poverty himself (*R*, 39–40, 50–51).

Although some say she lacked the common touch in technique and language,[2] she never lost her chief concern for the common man as subject, devoting a major part of her poetry to the poor. Arthur P. Davis thus describes her allegiance to the ordinary man:

> Gwendolyn Brooks is first of all the chronicler of the commonplace, of little men, of little actions. There are few, if any, truly heroic moments delineated in her poems. In fact, she seems to find a certain consolation in the little, the unheroic moment;
>
> > Exhaust the little moment. Soon it dies.
> > And be it gash or gold it will not come
> > Again in this identical disguise.
>
> . . . Gwendolyn Brooks's main concern is with the little people who do the usual and expected, who find joy in the familiar. In her assessment of modern man, it is the constant surprise of the ordinary that intrigues her; that is her ever-recurring theme.[3]

Gwendolyn's father was determined as a young man to finish school although no one else in his family had ever done so. The sacrifice was difficult, indeed, for much of his time was taken with farm chores. His reverence for education and for books very likely induced Gwendolyn to spend many hours reading as a child. During the Depression David furnished all the money for Gwendolyn's family by working as a janitor at McKinley Music Publishing Company. When times were difficult, the family ate beans. Memories of these experiences probably explain the references to beans and bean eaters in Miss Brooks's poetry, including the title of her third book of poetry, *The Bean Eaters*.

With a father like David Brooks, Gwendolyn and her brother, Raymond, were quite happy and secure in spite of the rough, "beany" times. They, like most children, would have feared dissension in the house much more than poverty and were content that their home was mostly peaceful. Her childhood home-life was filled with songs, family games, radio programs—reflecting much the same kind of family ties that prevailed in her father's boyhood homelife.

The other half of the peace and security achieved by the Brooks household came from Keziah Wims Brooks, Gwendolyn's mother. Gwendolyn's memory of her home as happy and comfortable, and indeed her perception of her father as powerful and secure, are due in large measure to the positive light which shone from Keziah's eyes. Her encouraging words and her belief in brightening the corner where she was often made rough places smooth. Keziah brought warmth, loving kindness, piano playing, fudge, cocoa, apricot pie, and other pleasant memorable experiences. She sang to her children and helped them with their homework, encouraging Gwendolyn in her intellectual pursuits and trying to remove every obstacle in the path of Gwendolyn's poetic career.

Keziah graduated from Topeka High School, attended Emporia State Normal, and later became a fifth-grade teacher at Monroe School in Topeka. In 1914 she met David Brooks and married him in 1916 in Chicago, Illinois, where he had gone to work. She came back to Topeka two and a half months before Gwendolyn was born and returned to Chicago just five weeks after Gwendolyn's birth.

As Gwendolyn's father had given her some of her more personal traits that evince themselves in her poetry, her mother provided the direct encouragement to pursue her poetic ambitions. She used to tell Gwendolyn, "You are going to be the lady

Paul Laurence Dunbar." She also did her utmost to see that Gwendolyn met the right people, such as James Weldon Johnson and Langston Hughes, in order to inspire and reassure her. Keziah Brooks did most of the housework, for instance, with the assistance of Raymond and her father so that Gwendolyn could do her writing. Gwendolyn remembers, however, having to help with dishes, dusting, sweeping, and laundry.

With her mother's guidance Gwendolyn had practice as a pre-schooler reciting pieces before audiences at Carter Temple Church. Her active mother trained groups of boys and girls ages ten to thirteen for special church programs. She asked Gwendolyn to write plays for them.

III   *Family and Homelife*

There were others besides Keziah and David who helped shape the life and career of Gwendolyn Brooks. Of them, perhaps Gwendolyn's maternal aunts are the most influential, but she had fond, rich memories of them all. With her aunts and uncles as with her father she remembers and was impressed with the seemingly ordinary aspects of their lives.

Aunt Eppie Small, the oldest of her mother's sisters, lived on a farm which Gwendolyn loved to visit in Kalamazoo, Michigan. Her aunt Gertrude was the most jovial and entertaining. She danced the Charleston and taught it to Gwendolyn. To Gwendolyn her Uncle Paul and Aunt Gertie were rich because he made fifty dollars a week while they lived in a "good" neighborhood and always had "good" things to eat. Aunt Ella and Uncle Ernest were poor but jovial. Uncle Ernest worked for the WPA and played cards and argued politics with her father, David. Aunt Ella was helpful and happy. Aunt Beulah was a high-school sewing teacher and made many, many dresses for Gwendolyn. In the summer she attended the prestigious University of Chicago. Considered the family queen, she chose not to marry in order to devote her life to helping the family. Gwendolyn remembers her as a very stylish dresser with powders, rouges and creams, trips, ice cream, toys, and games for nephews and nieces.

Even at the most ordinary of times Gwendolyn's early homelife appeared quite secure and encouraging. Holidays, however, in the Brooks household were especially endowed with the spiritual nourishment that accompanies wholesome familial interaction. The very patterns of behavior—the family traditions—were reassuring. At Christmas, for instance, there was a general effort to compact the joy of the holidays into the few days immediately before Christmas. The aroma and sounds of the season made the household exuberant. Among the regularized celebration, cleaning, cooking, and exchange of presents, books were a constant. Gwendolyn always received books, and she as regularly used to go behind the Christmas tree every year and read for hours by the tree light when the relatives were gone and the others were in bed. For Gwendolyn these were gifts that gave forever.

When she was a young child it did not bother Gwen that Santa Claus was white and that the holiday traditions of her family were European-oriented. Many years later Gwen was to take on a new perspective that would change the course of her life and writing. But there would be many stages of development for Gwen before this change.

Gwen spent her first four years of life in apartments with few playmates other than Raymond who was born when Gwen was sixteen months old. The lack of early playmates seems to foreshadow her social shyness as a preteen and teenager. Her energetic mother, however, saw that the children did not want for company. At three Gwen and her family lived in an apartment where some of the residents were given small gardening plots. Keziah loved to work in the garden and to exercise the children in the fresh air. They took walks for lunch in Jackson Park. At four Gwen and her family moved to what became the permanent Brooks home at 4332 Champlain Avenue. This house must have seemed much less confining than the apartments for it had a back porch, a hammock, and a sandbox.

It was often at the top of the steps on the back porch where Gwen did her best daydreaming. She loved the things of nature, especially the sky, its clouds, its red streaks; she says she was "infatuated with the sky." She was fond of imagining what the shapes of the clouds were. "Gods and little girls, angels, and heroes, and future lovers labored there, in misty glory or sharp grandeur." It was at a very early age that Gwendolyn, perhaps inspired by her daydreaming, showed an inclination to write. Her mother says that Gwen started rhyming at age seven but her first notebook was written when she was eleven. Gwen remembers "Forgive and Forget" as one of the first crude poems

(*R*, 40–56). She also at this early age was establishing a pattern of social behavior; she was often pensive and often alone. She either preferred the solitude or accommodated it by creating through her dreams and later through her poetry a world teeming with approachable, often likable people.

IV *Solitude: Mabbie on Mabbie*

Gwen at one time thought it would have been especially good for a poet to have grown up in the country and know all the birds, trees, and flowers. As an adult looking back, however, she feels that it is better to have grown up in the city, where she had an opportunity to know people. This explains perhaps why she features people and their concerns in her poetry. Responding once to the question of whether or not having grown up in the city had impeded her poetic career, she explained, "The city is the place to observe man *en masse* and in his infinite variety." Far from impeding her career, the city environment nourished.[4]

With all her concern about and preoccupation with people, Gwen was not popular as a child. Although she had friends, she felt inferior to everyone. Hence, her propensity to seek solitude. She was often ridiculed for liking to write and certainly considered odd for preferring writing to dancing. She considered her happiest moments to be those spent alone reading or writing. It was during this period that she was introduced to black literature by reading Countee Cullen's *Caroling Dusk*. Langston Hughes's *Weary Blues* made her realize the importance of writing about the everyday aspects of black life.[5]

Part of her shyness stemmed from Gwen's self-consciousness about being dark complexioned, for in the 1920s and 1930s color was an important social measuring rod among blacks, with the lightest skins the most highly valued. Therefore, she was usually "terrified and silent" at parties. Color became a recurrent theme in her poetry, like an early poem in *A Street in Bronzeville*, "The Ballad of Chocolate Mabbie," which tells the story of such a dark-skinned little girl's heartbreak at being rejected by the boy she loved in favor of "a lemon-hued lynx." "Mabbie on Mabbie . . ." reflects the little girl's thought about herself and the blame she placed on herself for the rejection she suffered from others.

Gwendolyn felt ostracism not only for being black with "bad hair," but also from the "wealthy" for being poor and from the poor for lacking the necessary "sass and brass," or the ability to fight. To make matters worse Gwen received numerous beautiful dresses from her Aunt Beulah, the high-school sewing teacher, further setting her apart from everyone—as Gwendolyn puts it "stamped doubly 'beyond the pale.'" There seemed to be some insidious conspiracy to assure her unpopularity. For her shy quietness she was labeled "a stuck up heifer." The boys called her "Ol' Black Gal." It is not as if Gwen did not want to be popular but she always felt that she would not have a chance—that everyone else would see her as inferior. All her outward doubts and self-effacement stemmed mainly from her concern with what others thought. Secretly in her own private world, Gwendolyn always felt that black was beautiful. She thought her arms, for instance, were a beautiful color—"charming"—and it hid mud. She knew, however, the social advantage of light complexion and a "Good Grade" of hair (implying fairly straight or curly).[6]

While the social pressures tended to sully the truly nice delights of school—chalk, lessons, crayon, watercolors, storytime, etc.—they also increased the amount of reading she did and led to her first juvenile but thoughtful and meditative poetry.

V *Early Milestones*

At age thirteen a milestone occurred when Gwendolyn discovered *Writer's Digest*. She was comforted to discover that there were many other writers experiencing the same beginners' anxieties and frustrations. During this year also her father gave her a desk which had been given to him at McKinley's, where he was a janitor. The desk, like the discovery of *Writer's Digest*, more firmly pointed Gwendolyn along the road to being a poet. With its many compartments the desk became a prized possession where she kept her papers and books. She kept a notebook there, too, after reading and being impressed with L. M. Montgomery's book on a Canadian girl who wrote and kept a notebook. She, of course, had books on Paul Laurence Dunbar in keeping with her mother's early announcement that Gwen would be the "lady Paul Laurence Dunbar." There is little wonder that Gwen from an early age had no doubt that she would be a poet.

Her family and social life further cooperated in the "conspiracy" to make her a poet by offering very few distractions. The few parties she attended, for instance, left her very uncomfortable. While the Charleston (taught to her by her aunt Gertrude) came in handy, as did the one-step and the two-step, it was insufficient. She lacked, she says, "the sass and brass" to be popular as a gradeschooler and teenager. Gwen could somehow never learn to "sashay with loud laughter, into the mysteries of the 'kissing game' " (*R*, 38, 57).

That at age fourteen Gwen preferred paper dolls to parties further illustrates her withdrawal. She increasingly fantasized and wrote perhaps as a substitute for popularity—for boyfriends. She had very few dates as a teenager or young woman. She "received" very few young men at her home and "went out" with still fewer. Her husband, whom she met when she was twenty-one, was her first "lover."

At Hyde Park High School she was ignored by the predominant whites. At Phillips High, an all-black school to which she transferred, she was not popular nor happy, because she could not dance or play kissing games; so she transferred again to Englewood High School. Gwendolyn remembers getting an A on a paper because she had done it in verse. She joined the journalism class and got along better in a mixed high school even if whites dominated and there were no black teachers.

Another milestone occurred when Gwendolyn was sixteen. She met two great black poets who inspired her a great deal. She had written to James Weldon Johnson to ask his opinion of some of her poetry. He had genuinely thrilled her by responding twice. Enthusiastically following his suggestions to read more modern poetry, she read Eliot, Pound, and Cummings. When Johnson failed to recognize her after giving a speech at her church some time later, Gwendolyn's mother was very disgruntled. His seeming coldness, however, was in sharp contrast to the warmth and graciousness of Langston Hughes whom she met a short time after that. He inspired Gwendolyn by reading some of her poetry on the spot and appraising it as showing talent.[7]

Gwendolyn's inner shyness was no doubt the basis for her unpopularity. As a young woman, she had friends and made efforts to get involved. Part of her "unshelling" occurred through her attendance for two years at Wilson Junior College where she joined several organizations. She was active in the NAACP Youth Council, broadening her interest and awareness of social, political, and racial events. At the age of twenty-one she was attending one of the NAACP Youth Council meetings at the

YMCA when she met Henry Blakely, who was to become her husband. When Gwendolyn first saw him he was standing with dignity in the YMCA door. She observed to her close friend, Margaret Goss (now Margaret Burroughs), "There is the man I am going to marry." Margaret, apparently not afflicted with any lack of "sass and brass," promptly yelled, "Hey, boy, this girl wants to meet you." Their common interest in writing drew them closer together.

VI *Married Life*

Gwendolyn and Henry's marriage for thirty happy years was filled with drives in old cars, picnics, movies, friends, sharing growth, children, and generally hard but good times. They shared each other's writings and readings and enjoyed spirited conversations, especially their breakfast talks. Henry, a man of intellect, imagination, and dynamic constitution, was the product of a fatherless home. Having been only thirteen and oldest of three sons when his father deserted his family, he was haunted by the memory of the desertion well into his adult life.

Explaining that she and Henry were happy despite their modest conditions, Gwendolyn says, "I believe a giggle or two may escape into the upper air of a Dachau, of a Buchenwald." Wherever they lived was enlivened and brightened by the sharing of their mutual interest—writing.

Their various residences included a honeymoon kitchenette apartment—bleak at first when compared to the rather comfortable Brooks home—a damp garage where Henry, Jr., contracted bronchopneumonia, and the kitchenette apartment at 623 East 63rd Street with its numerous mice and community bathroom. Doubtless these dwellings—often their more mundane aspects—inspired many of her poems, most notably, perhaps, "Kitchenette Building."

Another important source of inspiration for her poetry was her children, Henry, Jr., and Nora, born in 1940 and 1951, respectively. Again, Gwendolyn Brooks focused on the everyday activities—the charming little treasured incidents that grow more precious with the passing years are internalized and made immortal and universal in poetry. These everyday incidents along with Gwendolyn's concern for the well-being of her children and the children of other mothers in her circumstances are behind groups of poems like "Children of the Poor." These poems and others show that motherhood to her was no careless, capricious jaunt but a challenge worthy of serious reflecting, pondering. One can readily imagine, for instance, that "Life for My Child Is Simple, and Is Good" is about Henry, Jr. (*R*, 57–64). Gwendolyn had begun collecting items in a notebook for poems or for a book but has never developed it. Gwendolyn says that she had always intended to have children not only to enjoy raising and being proud of them with her husband but also to fulfill the beautiful capabilities of her body's glory.

If this last statement appears somewhat feministic, it may stem from Gwendolyn's early sensitivity to the rights and condition of women. This sensitivity spawned many lines and themes in her poetry. When coupled with her more general concern for the condition of black people, this theme makes a powerful presence in her poetry, as in "The Ballad of Pearl May Lee" (*World*, 44–47).[8]

Even with her concerns about the role of women in society, Gwendolyn loved and devoted much attention to her children and to her marriage. She wrote when she could find the time. She did very little writing during the first year of Henry, Jr.'s, life but wrote rather regularly after that. Henry, her husband, was encouraging but had to tolerate many inconveniences such as Gwendolyn's traveling and being away from the home. To Gwendolyn, on the other hand, marriage was quite demanding, requiring the woman constantly to put herself aside. In spite of the less than regal trappings and all her inconveniences, people felt that Gwendolyn and Henry's was a model marriage. They were separated, however, in December 1969. They felt that "separation—a dignified and mutually friendly one—is best." The separation would give them each time to consider new concepts so that life might be enhanced for both of them. Although when separated Gwendolyn indicated that she cherished the solitude and control of her life and that she would not marry again, the separation quietly ended in 1974 as mutually as it had begun.

VII *Launching a Career*

In the first happy years of marriage, Gwendolyn's writing career had been little more than a deep interest shared by her family and her husband. The first significant break came in 1941 when socialite Inez Cunningham Stark came to the South Side of Chicago to set up a writer's workshop. This wealthy white woman, writer, and scholar was evidently very much a rebel, for it was unheard of in 1941 that a member of the "Gold Coast" society from the North Side should instruct a class of black would-be poets. She came against the best advice of her friends, who said that she would be contaminated, robbed, raped, killed. Some of her detractors said that Negroes did not have the ability to create poetry. To her credit, Inez Stark disdained to be overly concerned with what many of her white peers thought.

Regarding herself not as a teacher but as a friend who liked poetry, she brought books to class, usually from her own fabulous library, and loaned them freely to any member of the class. A reader for *Poetry* magazine, Inez Stark gave Gwendolyn Brooks and her classmates an education in poetry. The whole class was taught incisiveness by criticizing each other's poetry and the poetry of established poets. Some of Gwendolyn's classmates were John Carlos, Margaret Burroughs, Margaret Cunningham, and Henry Blakely, serious and dedicated students, most of whom went on to become famous in their own right.

During this period of the early 1940s Gwendolyn was not producing much poetry for publication. When in 1943 she won the Midwestern Writers' Conference poetry award, she unknowingly was on her way. Emily Morison of Knopf congratulated Gwendolyn and asked her to send some poems when she had enough for a book. Hysterically Gwendolyn sent off about forty poems on love, war, "prejudice," nature, and other subjects. Emily Morison liked the "Negro poems," and hoped Gwendolyn would try again when she had a full collection. Very much encouraged but too shy to approach Knopf again, Gwendolyn worked up nineteen more "Negro poems" and sent them to Harper and Brothers.

Elizabeth Lawrence of Harper's advised her to take her time, but she could not. Miss Lawrence's approving letter advising Gwendolyn to wait two years prompted the anxious young poet to do just the opposite. Instead of waiting, she wrote assiduously and feverishly the eleven off-rhyme sonnets that precede "The Progress" and "The Sundays of Satin-Legs Smith." When Harper's sent a firm acceptance, Gwendolyn's family, neighbors, and "crowd went wild." Showing her elation about the publication, Gwendolyn says, "Finally, there came the little Harper-stamped package: ten author's copies of 'A Street in Bronzeville,' I took out the first copy. I turned the pages of the little thing, over and over, My Book" (*R*, 65–72).

Coupled with this momentous event was the launching of Gwendolyn's reputation by a sterling review of "A Street in Bronzeville" by prominent Iowa poet Paul Engle in the *Chicago Tribune*. Gwendolyn sums up the importance she attached to this review:

I'll never forget how my husband and I, returning from yet another Saturday night movie, bought the early Tribune and ripped it open to the book pages. "For Heaven's sake!" There, prominently situated, was the review that initiated My Reputation! Henry and I read the entire review on the midnight street, then waited in ecstasy for the bus. (*R*, 72)

The publication and the review more than adequately got her career off the ground. Congratulations were numerous. Of chief importance were those sent by well-known black poets: McKay, Cullen, J. W. Johnson. From Claude McKay: ". . . I want to congratulate you again on the publication of 'A Street in Bronzeville' and welcome you among the band of hard working poets who do have something to say. It is a pretty rough road we have to travel, but I suppose much compensation is derived from the joy of being able to sing. Yours sincerely." From Countee Cullen: "With every wish for your continued success, I am yours sincerely" (*R*, 201).

There was much other encouragement along the way. Elizabeth Lawrence, Miss Brooks's first Harper's editor, taught her much regarding publishing, as did Gene Young and Ann Harris, her second and third Harper's editors. Indeed Harper's was then and has remained very friendly and supportive.

In 1945 she received the *Mademoiselle* Merit Award. The following year she won the American Academy of Letters Award as well as Guggenheim Fellowships in 1946 and 1947. In 1948, riding the crest of her new popularity, Miss Brooks, in addition to writing poetry, began reviewing literary works under Van Allen Bradley, literary editor of the *Chicago Daily News*. Other reviews were written for Herman Kogan of the *Chicago Sun Times*, Bob Cromie of the *Chicago Tribune*, Hoyt Fuller's *Negro Digest*, the *New York Times*, and the *New York Herald Tribune*.

Although she enjoyed reviewing very much, she stopped because she felt she had not read sufficiently widely to be a very good reviewer. Among her most memorable reviews are those of Richard Wright's *Lawd Today*, Yasuari Kawabata's *Thousand Cranes*, Randall Jarrell's *The Lost World*, and Christine Arnothy's *It Is Not So Easy to Live*.

In 1949 she published her second book of poetry, *Annie Allen,* and received the Eunice Tietjens Memorial Award from *Poetry*. On the basis of this publication, the following year, 1950, Miss Brooks became the first black writer ever to win the Pulitzer Prize for literature. For the most part the reviews were very favorable indeed, reflecting the general high esteem that would be expected for a Pulitzer Prize–winning book of poetry. An anonymous review in the *New Yorker* in December 1949 praised Miss Brooks's "insight into the Negro dilemma in the Northern urban milieu. . . . Her sense of form which is basic, is still remarkable and she can pull a sonnet as tight as a bowstring—a loaded bowstring, at that." [9] While *Annie Allen* (1949) won a Pulitzer Prize and praise from some reviewers, it drew criticism from others. Many years later Don L. Lee (Haki Madhubuti) said, "*Annie Allen*, important? Yes. Read by blacks? No. *Annie Allen* more so than *A Street in Bronzeville* seems to have been written for whites" (*R*, 17).

The partly autobiographical novel *Maud Martha* (1953), a semi-poetic story of a young black woman in the ghetto, was less successful than her poems. It is a collection of tiny vignettes which Miss Brooks hoped would mesh. Miss Brooks feels that novels are not her proper metier partly because she takes the same care in selection of words for the novel as she does for a poem.

VIII   *The Party Era*

Between 1941 and 1949 social interaction through partying was almost as important as poetry to her development. Gwendolyn and Henry knew many famous painters, poets, pianists, dancers, actors, actresses, and photographers. Weekends for the South Siders meant parties at which they philosophized "into the dawn" over drinks, coffee, food. Great marathon discussions of social issues were common. In those days Gwendolyn and her crowd believed that if they talked long and intelligently enough, the world's problems would be solved. ". . . Society could be prettied, quieted, cradled, sweetened, if only people talked enough, glared at each other yearningly enough, waited enough" (*R*, 68).

The parties ran the gamut from the elaborate "spreads" or feasts, which were the center of Evelyn Ganns's fabulous parties held in her three-story house on Drexel to the casual "fall in" parties of Margaret Goss, who lived above a Michigan Avenue bar. Any personality might be there, white or black. One might see Paul Robeson, Peter Pollock, Frank Marshall Davie, Robert A. Davie, Eldzier Cortor, Hughie Lee-Smith, Charles White, Elizabeth Catlett, Marion Perkins (sculptor), Margaret Walker.

The best parties of Gwendolyn and Henry were given when they lived in their 623 East 63rd kitchenette apartment. Among their many parties was one given for Langston Hughes. Kindness and race pride were his trademarks whatever his endeavor. He believed in and expounded the beauty of blackness before it was yet fashionable. This wise, jovial, easy man squeezed with about a hundred other people into the two rooms of the apartment, and he was the merriest of all.

IX *Mentors, Heroes, and Helping Friends*

Some years later when Hughes dropped by unexpectedly, he was invited to share ham hocks, mustard greens, and sweet potatoes. "Just what I want!" exclaimed the noble poet. This ease and openness endeared him to Gwendolyn. He loved the young, helping and advising hundreds in their writing. Occasionally he devoted a column to Gwendolyn's work—before and after her books were published. He even dedicated his book of short stories *Something in Common* to Gwendolyn Brooks, making her very proud. His influence on Gwendolyn was subtle. He, too, loved and dealt with common man in his works. Gwendolyn says of this tendency, "Mightily did he use the street. He found its multiple heart, its tastes, smells, alarms, formulas, flowers, garbage and convulsions. He brought them all to his table-top. He crushed them to a writing-paste. He himself became the pen . . ." (*R*, 70–71).

Miss Brooks had always been thrilled when in the presence of her heroes and heroines or when she received recognition from them. Such was the case in 1950 when Miss Brooks, on her first

trip to the South, shared the speakers' platform with the formidable black educator Mary McCleod Bethune. Mrs. Bethune was at
first cold and unreceptive, perhaps reminding Miss Brooks of the
reception she had gotten from James Weldon Johnson many
years earlier. When Miss Brooks stepped to the podium and read
her poetry, however, Mrs. Bethune warmed up and was Miss
Brooks's most enthusiastic applauder, praising her graciously in
her speech.

With all the literary work—her writing and reviewing—and
the partying and the raising of her children one wonders where
Miss Brooks and her husband had time to cultivate friendships.
Somehow they managed to do so. Bob "Bookbeat" Cromie and his
wife, Alice, became very good friends of the Blakelys. There
were picnics, parties of course, plays, lunches, dinners, out-of-
town lectures, centennials, and other affairs together. Bob was
instrumental in getting Miss Brooks "little speakings" here and
there. Bob and Alice Cromie helped innumerable strugglers toward success, sharing their money and time with the Blakelys in
spite of personal and professional woes of their own and the up-
bringing of four children. Miss Brooks met many stars in the
Cromies' home—Claudia McNeill, Cleveland Amory, John
Drieske, Albert Memmi, Howard Greenfeld, Fran Loving (Mar-
lon Brando's brilliant writer sister).

Another notable helping friend among the many who con-
tributed to the launching and sustaining of Gwendolyn's career
was Robert H. Glauber, who had the courage in 1960 to give
The Bean Eaters a long, very complimentary review in the
Beloit Poetry Journal after other critics had remained silent for
months because the book was considered "too social" (*R*, 68–78).
The implications of the critics' silence seem clear: Miss Brooks's
"merits" as a poet depended on her "staying in line." Instead the
content was simple, implicitly more accusatory.[10] Miss Brooks
had always dealt with the conditions of black people, but she for
the most part had not previously enlarged the picture enough to
include the white man as a factor of the conditions. When she
did in *The Bean Eaters*, she was taken to task. Littlejohn chides
her militance, asserting that she is over-cultured and implying
that she lacks a real appreciation of the conditions of the poor.[11]

X   *Teaching*

In 1963 Mirron Alexandroff, president of Chicago's Columbia College, asked Miss Brooks to run a poetry workshop. She accepted and began her first real teaching job, although she had taught briefly at the University of Chicago under Frank London Brown's Union Leadership Program. Roosevelt University had refused to let her teach English because she lacked the degree. She taught creative writing classes also at Elmhurst College, Elmhurst, Illinois; Northeastern Illinois State College; University of Wisconsin in Madison as Rennebohm Professor of English. Here she taught poetry, fiction, and conducted writers' workshops. Miss Brooks attempted to give up teaching in June 1969, but accepted a position at City College of New York as distinguished Professor of the Arts. A slight heart attack on Christmas day in 1971 forced her finally to give up all her teaching activities.

Miss Brooks was considered a good teacher by her students largely because of the highly imaginative, diversified presentation and content of her classes. Through debates, lectures, round-robins, panel discussions, critiques, enactments of verse plays, and poetry-trades Miss Brooks taught such aspects of poetry as the sonnet (Shakespearean and Petrarchan) the ballad, blank verse, Japanese haiku and tanka, "beat" poems, and many more. Her assignments included attending plays, watching television literary programs, and hearing lectures by famous people. Then as today Miss Brooks advocated to the young aspiring writers to stay in school and to read as much as possible. In the late 1960s Miss Brooks began to expand and modify her teaching emphasis and method. Armed with the belief that poetry could be a vehicle for improving the lives of teenage street gang members, she began to hold poetry workshops and to sponsor writing contests in the predominantly black schools on the South and West sides of Chicago. She also supported and became active in Oscar Brown's Alley Theatre projects. Thus her teaching moved closer to the common people she wanted most to serve.

XI   *The Awakening*

Miss Brooks's life began to fill up with activities. Having published several books of poetry and received a number of prestigious awards and tributes, she had become a celebrity in a number of different circles. She certainly had achieved prominence and success among the literary establishment. As a speaker and reader of poetry she was accepted and revered by both whites and blacks. She was invited often to read her poetry and speak on college campuses and before black and women's groups. It is somewhat ironic that a shy woman who in earlier years had turned to writing partly to help endure the joylessness of unpopularity and who says that one reason she writes is that she is a poor speaker found herself extremely popular across the country as a speaker and reader among both blacks and whites in professional as well as in popular circles.

In 1967 during a circuit of such readings around the country Miss Brooks experienced a life-changing cultural shock. She had just left the virtually all-white South Dakota State College when she arrived in Nashville for another "reading" as part of a Black Writers' Conference at Fisk University, which is virtually all black. According to her, she was "loved" in South Dakota but only "coldly respected" at Fisk. The abrupt change was a revelation to her. The heroes of the conference were John Killens (novelist-director); David Llorens and Hoyt Fuller (editors); Ron Milner (playwright); John Henrik Clarke and Lerone Bennett (historians). But so angry was this group that even Bennett was berated for his association with *Ebony* and its ads for skin brighteners and its featuring of light-skinned women. Imamu Amiri Baraka emerged as the main hero with his "Up against the wall, white man"! He shared a very provocative reading with Ron Milner amid "intoxicating drumbeats." Miss Brooks and Margaret Cunningham (another "old timer") were amazed at what went on. The very bearing of the young people there was proud and angry. They denounced, protested, proclaimed, revealed so much and so vehemently that Miss Brooks was truly shocked. Fervor was not all the young people showed Miss Brooks. They showed her that they were keenly aware of the world around them. They revealed her own naiveté. Her own reception was lukewarm at best. She had come face to face with the black revolution's most prominent proponents. She was uneasily unprepared for the encounter. These young "tall walkers," as she calls them, spoke, sang, and read poetry about black power, black revolution, black nationhood with such an unwavering self-righteous zeal and utter disdain for conventional decorum and thought that Miss Brooks's reaction in her own terms was "agapeness," "almost hysterical," "blood-boiling surprise" (*R*, 79–85).

If one realizes that Miss Brooks considers herself to have "been asleep" before the revelation, one begins to understand why she was so shocked by the events at the Fisk Black Writers' Conference. During the 1940s and the 1950s she believed innocently in the basic goodness of man and of Christianity, that integration was the solution to the black man's problems, and that whites would eventually stop discriminating against blacks. Furthermore, the conversations at the big literary parties she attended in the 1940s had been about white writers and trends among whites. Having read very little serious writing by blacks, she speculates that even an attentive reading of Du Bois's *Souls of Black Folk* would have prepared her to a great extent. Haki Madhubuti (Don L. Lee) in his preface to Gwendolyn Brooks's *Report from Part One* says:

When you view Gwendolyn Brooks's works in the pre-1967 period, you see a poet, a black poet in the actual, (though still actively searching for her own definitions of blackness) on the roadway to becoming a conscious African poet or better yet a conscious African woman in America who chose poetry as her major craft.

She had thought of herself as a "Negro" before, not as black but had always been aware of the atrocities visited on blacks by whites. She had always been aware of the toleration, the condescension, patronizing kindness, segregation, humiliation, and while the American social climate was trying to tell her she was inferior, she had always the secret belief that it is good to be black.

After 1967 she became aware that other blacks feel that way and are not hesitant about saying it. She is now more conscious of her people and appeals to them for understanding rather than to white people. Her new awareness also prompts her to denounce integration in which she had before placed so much hope. She emphasizes, however, that blacks must be for black and not against white (*R*, 13–14, 44–45).

This change in her social perspective has caused a similar change in the perspective of Miss Brooks's poetry. She has noticed that black poets were paying much less attention to traditional

techniques and forms in poetry. She cites especially Etheridge
Knight, Carolyn Rodgers, Walter Bradford, James Cunningham,
Jewel Latimore, Ebon Dooley, Ornette Coleman, Leroy Neal,
and Leroi Jones (Amiri Baraka) as heroic poets who are mainly
concerned with bringing a message of black solidarity and black
self-consciousness to black people. While the traditional forms
and techniques have been forsaken, these poets have adapted
their poetry to traditional black forms like jazz music. She observed, for example, the fondness that many of these "new" black
poets have for the musician John Coltrane.[12]

Miss Brooks has also observed that as black writers disdain
adherence to traditional poetic forms, they also have shown little
concern any longer with white critics. She has come to feel—as
have other black poets—that white critics have demonstrated
their inability to understand and deal appropriately with black
poetry. Disregarding white critics, the new black poets between
1967 and 1968 felt very certain of the integrity and legitimacy of
their directions. Miss Brooks, having suddenly been shocked into
"awareness," now, like the new black poets, interprets the world
through new eyes. She remarks that since her awakening, even
reading the newspaper more intelligently informs her of much to
which she had before been oblivious.

In 1968, one year after her "loss of innocence," Miss Brooks
published her next major collection of poetry, *In the Mecca*. The
effect of the breakthrough on her poetry was immediately no-
ticeable. The revolutionary content of some of the poems of this
book sets them apart from her earlier writing, as does the directness and exclusiveness with which she addresses her messages to
black people. Yet it is clearly a continuation of the progression
toward her present philosophical stance. *In the Mecca* includes
one long poem by the same name which depicts life in an enor-
mous apartment building on Chicago's South Side. The teeming
tenement, the Mecca, was a real building and some of the characters are real individuals whose revolutionary fervor reflects
Miss Brooks's new awareness. Most of the remaining poems in
this book are revolutionary in nature, using the image of the
whirlwind and the harvest to convey the poet's sanction of the
struggle of black people for freedom and fulfillment.

Miss Brooks has been accused by some critics of abandoning
her "lyrical simplicity for an angrier, more polemical public
voice." To this charge she responds, ". . . No, I have not aban-
doned beauty, or lyricism, and I don't consider myself a polemical

poet." Acknowledging the profuse racial element in her poetry, she explains that it is organic, not imposed and that she writes about blacks as people, not as curios. "I'm a black poet, and I write about what I see, what interests me, and I'm seeing new things." [13] She feels that because the poet is a member of society, what affects society affects the poet. "So I, starting out, *usually* in the grip of a high and private suffusion, may find by the time I have arrived at a last line that there is quite some public clamor in my product." [14] She does not rely on mythology or any European tradition to express what she sees.

Miss Brooks further describes her change as a poet by explaining that while she is still concerned with words doing a good job, she wants to be uncompromising. She wants to write poetry that will be meaningful to common black people although she is not trying to be a "social force." [15] Miss Brooks says she wants to send an S.O.S. to "all black people in taverns, alleys, gutters, schools, offices, factories, prisons, the consulate, pulpits, mines, farms, thrones,—to teach, to entertain, to illumine. My newish voice will not be an imitation of the contemporary young black voice, which I so admire, but an extending adaptation of today's G.B. voice" (*R*, 183).

Miss Brooks believes that the differences in experience and therefore in perception can lead to a lack of appreciation by non-blacks for the feelings of black people as reflected by black poets. Appropriately, then, under her "And-then-they-ask 'Why-Are-You-Bitter?' Department" Miss Brooks lists this account:

In Ralph Ginzburg's *100 Years of Lynching* we are informed:

"When the two Negroes were captured, they were tied to trees and while the funeral pyres were being prepared, they were forced to hold out their hands while one finger at a time was chopped off. The fingers were distributed as souvenirs. The ears of the (victims) were cut off. Holbert was beaten severely, his skull was fractured and one of his eyes, knocked out with a stick, hung by a shred from the socket. Some of the mob used a large cork screw to bore into the flesh of the man and woman. It was applied to their arms, legs and body, then pulled out, the spirals tearing out big pieces of raw, quivering flesh every time it was withdrawn. Then the couple was burned 'at the stake,' killed."

An account of one of how-many Mississippi lynchings. (*R*, 200–201)

The memory of awareness of this kind of experience has been

kept alive by association with such common incidents as the following recounted by Miss Brooks:

In the long list of black people gaily killed by policemen, I want to remember the brilliant boy, a high school student in Nora's Hirsch High School graduating class, handsome Kenneth Alexander, killed before he could enter college, killed before he could make his major contribution to the world, merrily chased and merrily killed for nothing at all by a blackblood-thirsty uniformed murderer. We are tired of the best of our brilliance and of promise-in-embryo coming to early grief—chopped and pinned to official chests as medals. I cannot forget Kenneth, sitting shyly on the stage with his colleague-honorees, the only male among them, at the Honors Day ceremonies—then sampling peacefully of the tribute collation in the Hirsch reception room. He was going to *graduate*. And with his school's stamp of approval. He was building dreams. But what do you do with dreams in a grave? He did not know, and we who laughed with him and congratulated him and praised him did not know that in a few months he would be dead. . . . (*R*, 205–206)

The "new" Miss Brooks is admittedly less concerned about poetic form, using mostly free verse. She also feels it is silly to write about trees or something remote unless it has particular bearing on the present situation. Commenting on the black or the social content of poetry, she explains that the black poet may write about trees, but may be thinking of the ancestors lynched on the trees. Blacks perceive the same phenomena as whites but from different perspectives. The black writer probably has more to see in objects around him because more has happened to him. "He has the American experience and he also has the black experience; so he's very rich." [16] She writes about what she knows, drawing from the scenes and characters right around her in the ghetto. Certainly she has lost her concern for following certain poetic models like Eliot or Pound.

She has no desire to "preach" in her poetry but merely wants to present pictures of black life and thereby to teach. If she adheres to what she knows, it will be universal enough. Her premise as a poet remains to vivify the universal fact, modifying Whitman's "Vivify the contemporary fact." Miss Brooks, however feels that "the universal wears contemporary clothing very well." [17] Miss Brooks captures her feeling and those of other black poets about the reservoir of their subject matter—the black experience:

You are black. You see the black people. You love them. You want to put your arms around all of them—to say: "You are mine." You see the old woman with the crazy straw—the rusty little miss with one sock slipping down and her hair dull and wild—and, yes, you see the milk-colored cool young woman with the straight, brown-blond hair and the *natural* red in her cheek and the *natural* pink on her lip, and you remember that "one drop, *one drop* maketh a Negro" (some one hath said), that this has been received and ratified by black and white alike—and you accept her too—you know that the two of you must accept each other: you say, with a quizzical but genial bewilderment, "You're mine." And Blackness—the red of it, the milk and cream of it, the tan and yellow-tan of it, the deep-brown middle-brown high-brown of it, the "olive" and ochre of it—Blackness marches on. . . . (*R*, 213–14)

People—the characters—are the most important aspect of her poetry. She is an observer of people and gifted recorder of their lives through her poetic vignettes.

After 1967 Miss Brooks had not only a new awareness but a new direction to her life and with it a new freedom. She began to sponsor writing contests in the elementary and secondary schools as well as at colleges and universities in and around Chicago. In 1968 Miss Brooks was named poet laureate of Illinois, succeeding the late Carl Sandburg. But characteristic of the new Miss Brooks, she has made the post a working one—a "contributing thing"—a service to the young. She had not wanted to be "tied" down to an office or to have official duties. She felt the poet laureate should do more than wear a crown—should be of service to the young. She calls the honor a "pleasant salute—a smile." [18] In 1970 she started the Annual Poet Laureate Award of $500 for the two best high-school poets.

Miss Brooks's newfound freedom and awareness include her views on many aspects of civil rights and race relations. She is very supportive of the black man's general struggle to achieve his civil rights. She feels, furthermore, that because black women are needed by black men as they fight for their rights and manhood, a separate black women's liberation movement should be postponed and that black women should be beside their increasingly assertive men, not organized against them. On the other hand, Miss Brooks believes that "personhood precedes femalehood" and that the black woman cannot afford to endlessly brood over the black man's "blonde, blues, and blunders." The black woman has a place in the world with wrongs that need to be righted *with* her man if possible, but if not, without him (*R*, 204).

Another evidence of her serious new commitment to blackness and of her identification with it is her switching from Harper and Row—by whom she had had all her works published since 1945—to Detroit's Broadside Press, directed by Dudley Randall. The purpose of the press was to provide a ready means of publication for young black writers. In 1969 Miss Brooks had *Riot* published by Broadside Press, followed by *Family Pictures* in 1970. In 1971 *The World of Gwendolyn Brooks* was the last of her books to be published by the New York house she had long been associated with. Another of her books to be published by Broadside Press in 1972 was *Report from Part One*, Miss Brooks's autobiography, which she had always intended to have Harper's bring out. Her new awareness, she contends, is like the Jews' identification with Israel and the identification of the Chicago Irish with Northern Ireland. It is nothing extraordinary for a poet to identify with his people. Art, she feels, should be used for liberation—not decoration.[19]

The notion that writing alone is not enough coincides well with her new "militant" or "functional" poetry. In "Young Africans" she says:

> If there are flowers, flowers
> must come out to the road. Rowdy!—
> knowing where wheels and people are,
> knowing where whips and screams are,
> knowing where deaths are, where the kind kills are.
> (*Family Pictures*, 18)[20]

Symbolic of her new freedom was her first flight on an airplane in 1971. She had always been afraid of flying but now has no fear. She says it is good to be airborne.[21]

XII   *Africa: A Glimpse of Home*

The significant general change in Miss Brooks's life and writing was further exemplified by her trip to East Africa in 1971. She was overwhelmingly happy to be in Africa among the Africans with their rich colors and marvelous outfits and proud to see the resemblances of the Africans to the blacks in Chicago. Very possessive about Africa belonging to blacks, she was refreshed by the apparent "wholesomeness" of the young men. Their walk, for instance, was no "pimp" walk but "usually full of fresh air and bounce!" She likewise admired the shy strength of African girls. Interested in the opinions and feelings of Africans toward blacks of the United States, Miss Brooks noticed that while she thinks of Africans as brothers, Africans sometimes see Afro-Americans (blacks) as threats or seem to have forgotten American blacks. Sad because she had been separated from the Africans in culture, especially language, she observed a mystique but felt left out because she could not speak the language. In an effort to bridge the cultural gap, she learned a little Swahili. This great loss which Miss Brooks feels evinces itself in her poetry as the theme of the estrangement from "home."

Her advocacy for the solidarity of black people is reflected in her long-felt need for a Black World Day celebration based on a traditional African holiday to honor the great strength and achievements of black people. This day she proposes could be an alternative to commercial-oriented Christmas. This holiday should abound with red, black, green decorations and festivities starting around December 26. Red should symbolize bloodshed; black, the black nation; and green, the land for nation-building and faith in our young. Moreover, there should be African joy and shouting—but also African calm. Overall should prevail an air of "gaudy wholesomeness" of costumery, jewelry, African foods—figs, oranges, vegetables, etc.—much of the warm hand-shaking which is so important in Africa (R, 45–46).

XIII Surprised Queenhood

Having written her books, developed a new awareness, gone to Africa, and received awards and acclaim, Miss Brooks finds herself enjoying a state of "surprised queenhood" among black people. She continues to write and to give readings of her poetry. She continues her work with young black artists and maintains her close association with Broadside Press. She considers her friend and publisher, Dudley Randall, editor at Broadside, to be a man of substance, talent, innocent kindness, and strength. He, along with Haki Madhubuti (Don L. Lee), joins Gwendolyn Brooks in a "random triumvirate" to accomplish frequent literary-critical jobs together. She describes Madhubuti as a recognized star for black people—young and old. He is "uncompromising, serious, consistent with warmth inside a mail of necessary cold."

As her esteem rose among blacks, it also took on a new legitimacy among the white literary establishment, including academics. Her previously described teaching experiences and her many college campus speaking engagements have enhanced her popularity a great deal. Having never received a college degree, she had longed for a single honorary doctorate. In 1964 Columbia College awarded her the Doctorate of Humane Letters. Mike Alexandroff, who had helped her start as a teacher, made the award. But this was only the beginning. Lake Forest College, Elmhurst College, Skidmore College, the Illinois Institute of Technology, Mundeleine College, Lewis College, Loyola University, Southern Illinois University, the University of Wisconsin, Northwestern University, Millikin University, Western Illinois University, and DePaul University all followed with similar awards. Miss Brooks takes special pride in the black students at Western Illinois University naming their Black Student House the Gwendolyn Brooks Black Cultural Center in her honor in March 1970.

Recognition and queenly prominence have come in other forms, too; Miss Brooks's impressive list of tributes includes mention in *Esquire*'s One Hundred Most Important People in the World, *Ebony*'s One Hundred Most Influential Black Americans, *Ladies Home Journal*'s Seventy-five Most Important Women in America, *Mademoiselle*'s Ten Women of the Year, *Town and Country*'s Who's Who in Chicago, *Panorama*'s Sixty-two Best People in Chicago, *McCall*'s Seventy-one People Who Made a Difference in 1971.

The queenhood, the new awareness, the tributes, the awards have not essentially changed Miss Brooks. She still seems basically shy and uncomfortable in some public situations, perhaps desiring as in the past the refuge of solitude. Once while receiving yet another honor by attending President Lyndon Johnson's Presidential Scholar's reception at the White House, she felt the old discomfort she used to feel in grammar school or at teenage parties. Having gone "beautifully gowned in blue chiffon" while the other ladies were in knits, tweeds, and linen did not ease her anxiety any. She was tongue-tied and speechless when the president smiled at her. Being somewhat over-awed by the situation, she made what she considers another mistake. She left early; in fact, she was the first to leave. She found out later that one must never leave before the presidential party. Of this she said, however, that "at a certain moment in social proceedings I am on FIRE to leave; I have a leaving-FIT" (*R*, 196–200). But on December 28, 1969, two years after her "awakening," no such "leaving fit" was evident as Miss Brooks received her "most stirring tribute" at her night of honor at the Afro-Arts Theatre. She had made the necessary adjustments in her perspective and felt most at ease with her black brothers and sisters. This new rapport and esteem stem partly from her new awareness which put her more in line with the reality of the present black situation. It is, however, in large part due to a new awareness by black people of the rich black beauty that her poetry has always possessed.

CHAPTER 2

The World of Gwendolyn Brooks

I Raw Materials

THE shy, quiet dignity of Gwendolyn Brooks seems somehow appropriate for one born in Topeka, Kansas, on June 7, 1917. Yet her unquestionably incisive observations and urbane poetic renderings of the ghetto life around her fittingly bespeak her rearing from the age of five weeks on Chicago's South Side. From early in her career with the publication of *A Street in Bronzeville* in 1945 and the winning of the Pulitzer Prize for Poetry for *Annie Allen* in 1950, her poetry has been a star to many a kind of "wandering bark" and has brightened corners near and far, old and new, revealing the remote to be familiar after all and the familiar to be more profound than had been imagined.

Some critics, mainly blacks, feel that this early success came partly at the expense of her not paying proper attention to matters that concern blacks and that she was excessively oriented toward appealing to whites.[1] Some white critics feel, on the other hand, that the later part (since 1967) of her career has suffered artistically because of an inordinate amount of attention given to racial matters as opposed to those matters with more "universal" appeal.[2] While it is true as some point out that Gwendolyn Brooks has changed over the years of her career, she has never been as naive as some believe, nor has she become as polemical as others believe. Far more significant, however, than any change in Gwendolyn Brooks is that her trenchant vignettes have accurately reflected the changing attitudes of blacks for the past three decades. Consistently a portraitist of black people, she unavoidably deals with race and racism in her poetry but in the best tradition of the artist drawing the scenes that he knows best. The startling, fresh irony with which she depicts conditions in the black community likewise has been a consistent feature of her poetry. She is fond, for instance, of pointing out the paradoxes that abound in the disparity between the American creed and the American reality.

In revealing these paradoxes she draws from the black experience employing four major themes: death, the fall from glory, the labyrinth, and survival. The parallels between the vignettes and various aspects of black life show that the themes constitute a mimesis of black life and are rooted in the psychological and social realities of the black experience. There is a great deal of overlapping, so that their order of appearance is a very rough one determined by emphasis rather than any precise stopping and starting.

With their roots in the traditional and the present realities of the black experience, the social themes in the poetry of Gwendolyn Brooks are sufficiently esoteric in their expression to warrant general explanation and definitions of their salient features and of the methods of their presentation. As a writer of lyrics, ballads, sonnets, and other short poems, Miss Brooks includes virtually no dramatic dialogue or plots in the usual sense; yet through the body of her poetry she manages to depict as a coherent, unified story every major social aspect of the black experience from former African freedom through the trials of slavery to the present-day struggles for dignity and equality. Her artistic prowess helps her poetry to be an effective means of expressing social themes. The artful ambiguity and richness of Miss Brooks's versatile, potent verse allow for the expression of profound thoughts and subtle emotions.

This complexity of expression allows, on the one hand, an esoteric understanding by the readers who share the black experience just as familiarity with the social and political conditions of Elizabethan England afforded the audiences of Shakespeare's plays an inherent insight into their nuances of meaning. For those readers not sharing the black experience there is no frame of reference for understanding many of the allusions that are made, especially those made to the black man's social condition. On the other hand, the complexity of Miss Brooks's poetry also allows an exoteric approach to the statements about and allusions to subjects based on the human experience and having no apparent special connection to the black man's social predicament.

Miss Brooks's vignettes fit harmoniously into a large context, a comprehensive history. Otherwise they remain merely simple pictures of black life, as they must to those who lack familiarity with the black experience. Each vignette is presented on a common stage with a common backdrop. The various stock characters take turns, as do some of the props, like variations on familiar themes. Generalizations about black experience situations are part of a vast group knowledge or intelligence, and black folks have already been, for the most part, wherever the vignettes take them. Yet viewing one's history and one's present conditions through the wise eyes of the persona is more enlightening than life itself because the truths revealed are less avoidable, less dilutable, and less manipulable than those encountered in life situations, but not less true. Miss Brooks's poetry can be thought of as "cassette" poetry that, when fitted into a larger familiar and complementary context, enlivens the whole scene, producing a heightened sense of unity and coherence about the black experience in particular and a better perspective of human nature in general.

Miss Brooks presents the black experience as a story but not necessarily in chronological order. The various social themes of death, the fall from glory, the labyrinth, and survival represent different but interrelated states in the story of the experience of the black man of the United States. The order in which the themes are discussed in this study will follow roughly the order in which they are introduced and emphasized in the total body of Miss Brooks's poetry. While the themes are for the most part conterminous entities, there is a certain logic to the order in which they appear. In her poetry, Miss Brooks first depicts the most prevalent social reality of the black man's present state as spiritual death. Second, her poetry shows that it is from the vantage point of death that the black man views his former glory and freedom, the loss of which constitutes his spiritual death. Beyond the profuse indications of the mere existence of death, the poetry next focuses on the most salient characteristic of the black man's effort to escape his peculiar kind of hell in the United States—the groveling confusion of the labyrinth. Finally, the theme of survival, with its components of restraint, militance, and rebirth offers an answer to death by envisioning the black man's enduring to solve the labyrinth and reclaim former glory.

II *Poet of the Black Experience*

The death that the poet is most concerned about is the spiritual death of the black man. However, because the best image for spiritual death is physical death, her poetry contains many references to death and dying. Many other more subtle images of death abound throughout her poetry. Almost any concrete image in the black urban environment can be used to suggest death. For instance, the dwellings in "Southeast Corner" and "Kitchenette Building" evoke death as images of negative displacement and stifling squalor. "The Birth of a Narrow Room" presents a picture of birth in a grave, the black setting, as one feels the pinch of suppression translated into squalor and vice versa. Flowers, the seasons, and ice are but a few of the many other concrete images Miss Brooks uses to evoke the idea of death.

Because in Miss Brooks's poetry death is usually presented as the present condition which has replaced former glory, she often speaks of life as hell, implying that there has been a "fall" from glory, a paradise lost. This sense of having fallen heightens the effect of a spiritual death of the suppliants groveling in earthly hell. The numerous references to "returning" and "home" and "remembering" in her poems indicate Miss Brooks's awareness of the black man's sense of having fallen from a high position. "My Dreams, My Works, Must Wait till after Hell" illustrates the heavy implication of going back to a former position of power. Negative displacement, the displacement of something relatively good with something of less worth, is used often to suggest the fall from glory. In the apparently innocent "The Vacant Lot," a sense of nothing replacing something is depicted. Beyond this general displacement, the African son-in-law in this poem further communicates a sense of displacement. He should, after all, have been king. Instead his wife is a whore. But majesty is only gone for the day and will return. Blacks are displaced people, and lingering subconsciously in many blacks is the dream of inheriting the "throne" and the hope that as "trouble don't last always" so whoring, squalor, and other misery will be gone forever when majesty returns. Much the same kind of point can be made about "Southeast Corner" and numerous other poems.

The labyrinth is a term used here to refer to Miss Brooks's concern about the confusion and uncertainty of the black man in finding his way home. The indecision of the black man as expressed in such poems as "One Wants a Teller in a Time Like This," "Truth," "People Protest in Sprawling Lightless Ways," and "Men of Careful Turns, Haters of Forks in the Road" leads to an inner conflict concerning the choice between restraint and militance.

Because misery is still being wreaked upon the characters of Miss Brooks's poetry (black and occasionally women), the characters are caught up in a perpetual denouement shared by the author-persona and by the reader whose experiential background provides him with enough insight to make use of the objective correlatives in the poems. Miss Brooks's vignettes continually awaken the reader and herself to discover and rediscover in intermittent epiphanies their respective roles in the overall situation.

One repeated epiphany in the labyrinth is the discovery that the black man's most inescapable reality is the unreality of the white man's way of thinking about him. The basic dilemma as shown in Miss Brooks's poetry is that the black man must generally either fight and die or survive by submitting, which is spiritual death. "The Ballad of Rudolph Reed" exemplifies both choices—Rudolph choosing to fight and die, his wife to submit (though oakenly) and survive. It should be pointed out that there are two kinds of submission. One is the kind that is exemplified here by the wife of Rudolph Reed where the subdued knowingly and stoically bear their fate. Another kind of submission occurs when a character fails to face the reality of his situation either through ignorance, as in "Strong Men, Riding Horses," or through outright escape, as in "We Real Cool."

III *Survival with Dignity*

Survival being one of the most basic human motivations, it is not surprising to see characters in Miss Brooks's poetry do whatever is necessary to survive. Very few people are simple enough to play dead seriously and self-consciously. Most of them devise subconscious ways of escaping from the horror of their reality. Miss Brooks captures the many complexities of the characters by having them engage in fantasies, dreams, alcohol, sex, or anything which can diminish the glare of the provoking insult and enable them to survive as in "The Sundays of Satin-Legs Smith."

Miss Brooks's poetry is replete with examples of people using devices to camouflage the realities of life, but the reader is afforded glimpses of the ragged edges of the basic oppression which occasionally appears with sudden, brief directness and clarity. Forced to accept the various roles the suppliant must play in order to survive and still retain some dignity, the black man seeks to manipulate the realities of life. These roles played by black men find expression ranging from spirituals to sit-ins. Sometimes when the suppliant roles become so intolerable that survival of dignity becomes more important than survival of limb, the black man resorts to physical violence as a means of expression. These roles become intolerable whenever all the devices which hide the insult are stripped away.

Militance is the result of the black man's raging "against the dying of the light." The light being in this case his spiritual life, the protagonist strikes out "ungentle" against the night. In the poems of *Riot* Miss Brooks captures the desperate feeling of a people compelled to act sacrificially. The supreme sacrifice has to do with survival of the human spirit, not the body. She refers, for instance, to a riot as the Phoenix with which new life rises. These lines about those slain in riots communicate the essence of the sacrifice:

> There they came to life and exulted;
> The hurt mute.
> Then it was over.
> The dust, as they say, settled. (*Riot*, 20)

Of course, the truth that overt black militants do not live long but rather "die soon" can be amply documented by United States history and is illustrated by poems like "Medgar Evers" and "Malcolm X." But Miss Brooks shows not only overt militance but also the kind that can be reconciled with survival—that kind which is not too conspicuous and certainly not too offensive. "People Protest in Sprawling Lightless Ways" affords an example.

The opposing yet complementary quality which helps tame the insult is the faith that through stoic perseverance, or survival, black hell becomes a sacrificial experience enabling the eventual return to glory. Among the poems that show the stoical approach to the black experience are "The Bean Eaters," "The Parents:

People Like Our Marriage Maxie and Andrew," and "The Ballad of Rudolph Reed."

While Hamlet had the choice of being or not being, Rudolph Reed, exemplifying a black man forced to choose self-sacrifice, simply could not be, at least not in any role other than that prescribed by society. Implicit in this poem and others by Miss Brooks is the absurd reality that the black man has violated a moral law simply by existing, particularly when he transgresses society's sacrosanct notions about his "place." This kind of tacit message gives great ironic effect to some of her quiet, subtle poems such as "Bronzeville Woman in a Red Hat Hires Out to Mrs. Miles."

Language, thought, and emotion in subtleness and profoundness are chief ingredients in the creation of character. Therewith Miss Brooks is able to draw some of her characters from only a few lines. Whether etched in fire like Rudolph Reed or puffed out in fragrant vapors like Satin-Legs Smith, they are familiar, memorable, and complex. Miss Brooks's poetry draws from domestic or bourgeois settings, with its protagonists existing among the common people. Almost without exception her characters and situations are drawn from life on Chicago's predominantly black South Side, which she sometimes refers to as "Bronzeville." [3] More to the point, the poems nearly always deal with some negative aspect of life among the poorest black people, whether it be their squalor, overcrowding, duplicity, callousness, fear, ignorance, despair, or others. Her personae's points of view most often involve an omniscient observer who closely identifies with these poor blacks. [4] Even when whites or middle-class blacks are included, the tone of the poem is in favor of the lowly black that encounters them, as in "A Man of the Middle Class," "Bronzeville Woman in a Red Hat Hires out to Mrs. Miles," "Lovers of the Poor," and "Beverly Hills, Chicago."

Miss Brooks's poetry presents good pictures of the black man as hero, progressing and retrogressing in the various stages of the black experiences as he attempts to cope with his environment. Like the best of ancient Greek and Elizabethan tragedy, her poetry very often employs death as an indication of the seriousness of the action imitated. Other social themes included in her poetry depict the black man's sense of a fall from glory, his groveling confusion, his desperate attempt to strike back at his malefactor, his soberer compromise for the sake of survival, and the intimations of spiritual rebirth. The task of this study is to provide insight on the poet's life and career and to show how the poet realizes the aforementioned social themes in individual poems.

CHAPTER 3

Death

THE writer who uses the theme of death with integrity borrows at once elements of appeal and repulsion, individuality and universality. Death as a literary theme has perhaps as much evocative power as any other because it seems to be variously the escape from an unpleasant life or a grim joke of which man is the butt. The sheer frequency with which death appears in Miss Brooks's poetry indicates its importance in her thinking. She reveals death as it patrols the most commonplace settings, overseeing the activities and preying on the bodies and souls of black men. In her vivid pictures of black life Miss Brooks captures the black man's preoccupation with the avoidance of the physical and spiritual death that pervade his environment. Though their immediate literal reference is to war, "Piano after War" and "Mentors" from *A Street in Bronzeville* provide fitting epitomes of the poet's early emphasis on death, illustrating the death thought's intrusion even in the midst of life's lighter, more pleasant moments. While the first sonnet, "Piano after War," indirectly alludes to this intrusion, the second sonnet, "Mentors," addresses it squarely:

> On a snug evening I shall watch her fingers,
> Cleverly ringed, declining to clever pink,
> Beg glory from the willing keys. Old hungers
> will break their coffins, rise to eat and thank.
> And music, warily, like the golden rose
> That sometimes after sunset warms the west,
> Will warm that room, persuasively suffuse
> That room and me, rejuvenate a past
> But suddenly, across my climbing fever
> Of proud delight—a multiplying cry.
> A cry of bitter dead men who will never
> Attend a gentle maker of musical joy.

Then my thawed eye will go again to ice.
And stone will shove the softness from my face.

For I am rightful fellow of their band.
My best allegiances are to the dead.
I swear to keep the dead upon my mind.
Disdain for all time to be overglad.
Among spring flowers, under summer trees,
By chilling autumn waters, in the frosts
Of supercilious winter—all my days
I'll have as mentors those reproving ghosts.
And at that cry, at that remotest whisper,
I'll stop my casual business. Leave the banquet.
Or leave the ball—reluctant to unclasp her
Who may be fragrant as the flower she wears,
Make gallant bows and dim excuses, then quit
Light for the midnight that is mine and theirs. (*World*, 52–53)

Blacks are aware of this awesome and sinister supervision and that it is largely man-imposed. The poetry deciphers the manifestations of this awareness and thereby records its psychological and sociological effects. It is in the context of these effects and their manifestations that the theme of death is considered in the poetry of Gwendolyn Brooks.

The black man's preoccupation with the avoidance of death stems from his fear and hatred for the man-imposed environment full of physical and spiritual death. The instances of untimely physical death among blacks are so much higher per capita than they are among the general population that it is obvious that blacks are victims of the disadvantages foisted upon them by the larger society. Deaths and the fear of death due to malnutrition, child-disease, infant mortality, lead poisoning, rat bites, lynching, capital punishment military service, inadequate medical attention, suicide, drug abuse, alcohol abuse, murder, and other causes play a much more important role in the everyday lives of blacks than in those of whites and, therefore, affect their psyches differently.[1]

Instances of spiritual death, on the other hand, are not so apparent, although they may be just as pervasive or even more pervasive than the instances of physical death. While one has little trouble accepting that physical death is the end of physical life, spiritual death is more difficult to define. It is the cessation, curtailment, stifling of spiritual life or of certain qualities which are as vital to the life of the human spirit as heartbeat and brainwaves are to the life of the body. Much of the subject matter of Miss Brooks's poetry is the absence of these essential qualities. Some of the elements commonly considered to be essential to spiritual life are dreams, hope, love, pride, freedom, a sense of power, security, and a positive identification with one's history. Contributors to spiritual death such as poor education, welfare, subsistence, unemployment, cultural deprivation, and police brutality are frequently subjects in her poetry. Because of the proximity of the subjects to images of physical death and the manner in which the subjects are presented, it is reasonable to conclude that the poet is indeed discussing the pervasive struggle of the black man to ward off spiritual death.

I *The Vehicle of Physical Death*

The references in Miss Brooks's poetry to physical death have the effect of setting the appropriate tone for ghetto life. The black man's unwilling intimacy with physical death is often reflected in Miss Brooks's poetry by her employment of such subjects as murders, funerals, and war. It should be pointed out that physical death per se is hardly ever the subject of her poems. Very often it is used merely as a vehicle to connote spiritual death. Most notable examples of poems that are ostensibly related to murder are "Medgar Evers," "A Bronzeville Mother Loiters in Mississippi. Meanwhile, a Mississippi Mother Burns Bacon," and "Malcolm X." The objects of death in two of these poems were well known people whose murders were felt very deeply by the black people in this country.

Expending notably little attention in "Medgar Evers" on the murderer and his kind ("and palsy" illustrates the fear that they had of the surprising, unequivocating courage of Evers), Miss Brooks deals with physical death as one of the choices that Evers knew he had:

> The raw
> intoxicated time was a time for better birth or
> a final death.

"Intoxicated" suggests a recklessness, a disregard for survival—

which is a break with the past. This break is further emphasized
by the stanza:

> old styles, old tempos, all the engagement of
> the day—the sedate, the regulated fray—
> the antique light, the Moral rose, old gusts,
> tight whistlings from the past, the mothballs
> in the Love at last our man forswore.

Ironically, this "final death" is not the physical death but the
spiritual death he could create if he did not face almost certain
physical death by arranging "to fear no further." By meeting
physical death with dignity and courage, Evers contributes to
a "better birth" for black people: "he leaned across tomorrow
. . . holding clean globes in his hands." This poem dramatizes
what is a common assumption among blacks: that a black man
is in danger of death unless he stays in his place. Now, "his
place" is a man-defined one and as such is intolerable to the
point that staying in it constitutes spiritual death. We can be
sure that Medgar Evers was aware of his peril, for Miss Brooks
refers not only to his forswearing of this traditional place and its
safety but also to the bribery attempts:

> Medgar Evers annoyed confetti and assorted
> brands of businessmen's eyes

—and the threats:

> The shows came down: to maxims and surprise.
> And palsy. (*World*, 410)

In "Malcolm X" the word "was" in the last line and the history
of the man Malcolm are all that are necessary to make this poem
a confirmation of the assertion that black heroes often meet with
untimely deaths. The poem is evidence that, once having chosen
the route of fulfilling the concept of manhood, the black man is
in great danger of physical death. The reference to the "hawk-
man's eyes" refers not only to maleness but beyond that to his
keen perception and broad perspective. He fully knew what his
fate would be.

In both the previous poems the murdered transgressed the
boundaries of their "place" with their eyes open, fully aware and

prepared to take the awful consequences. By contrast the inno-
cence of Emmett Till is emphasized in "A Bronzeville Mother
Loiters in Mississippi. Meanwhile, a Mississippi Mother Burns
Bacon":

> He should have been older, perhaps.
> . . . .
> . . . the Dark Villain was a blackish child
> Of fourteen, with eyes still too young to be dirty,
> And a mouth too young to have lost every reminder
> Of its infant softness.
> That boy must have been surprised!

Again Till is referred to as "That little foe" and the description
of the murder itself stresses the innocence of Till:

> the blood, the cramped cries, the little
> stuttering bravado,
> The gradual dulling of those Negro eyes,
> The sudden, overwhelming *little-boyness* in that barn.
>   (*World*, 317–23)

One point here is that the old formula holds true; that trans-
gressing the boundaries of "place" is punishable by death,
whether the transgression is done out of awareness or innocence.

Unlike Medgar Evers and Malcolm X, Rudolph Reed was no
idealist, nor was he innocent in the same way as was Emmett
Till. He was instead an uncompromising pragmatist concerned
about the well-being of his family. This concern conflicted with
his inability to bend. Being "oaken," Reed, though not looking
for a fight, would never be able to run from one. "The Ballad of
Rudolph Reed" provides an example of yet another dimension
of the traditional formula which prescribes death for those black
men who cross the barriers associated with "place" in United
States society.[2]

Rudolph Reed reacted to his stifling environment and was
killed. He obviously chose certain physical death over spiritual
death which he would have tolerated had he continued to be
stoned without striking back.

> Patience ached to endure.
> But he looked, and lo! small Mabel's blood
> Was staining her gaze so pure.

> Then up did rise our Rudolph Reed
> And press the hand of his wife,
> And went to the door with a thirty-four
> And a beastly butcher knife. (*World*, 362)

Reed knew he was to die, and when he pressed his wife's hand he was saying goodbye. Furthermore, his wife knew that he would die, but knew that he had to go out and fight or not be Rudolph Reed. This mutual awareness and agreement to the terms of death by Reed and his wife bespeak of profound love, respect, and pride that they felt for each other: "Her oak-eyed mother did no thing / But change the bloody gauze." One is impressed with the idea that life will carry on and that Reed's dream of providing a comfortable home may be much more realized than if he had not been willing to die for it.

Still another ballad is used to relate death by murder, and again the murder is related to a black man's transgressions of "place." "The Ballad of Pearl May Lee" depicts Sammy violating the sex taboo for which again the penalty is death. In this poem, however, the tone is not so accusing toward the murderers as in the other poems. The reason is that Pearl May Lee is torn between grief and spite and feels that Sammy got what he deserved:

> You paid with your hide and my heart, Sammy boy,
> For your taste of pink and white honey.
> . . . .
> Oh, dig me out of my don't-despair.
> Oh, pull me out of my poor-me.
> Oh, get me a garment of red to wear.
> You had it coming surely. (*World*, 44–47)

The idea is that Sammy had committed murder, too. For this he deserves to die. He had always preferred light-skinned girls.[3] The guilt of the whites in the murder is almost uncontested because it is secondary here. Pearl May Lee is spiritually dead, dressed in a "garment of red." She has chosen the high life, the extravagances of which in the black ghetto are often supported by death-bringing activities. Also, in the eyes of Pearl May Lee, Sammy was already spiritually dead, having suffered, according to Arthur P. Davis, "a spiritual mutilation as real as the physical one he suffers at the hands of the mob."[4]

The death of Pepita in "In the Mecca" represents another kind
of murder in the black community. Like Emmett Till, she is
innocent but is killed by a black with a mind perverted as the
result of trying to twist free from the manacles of oppression.
Jamaican Edward is both victim and victimizer:

> Hateful things sometimes befall the hateful
> but the hateful are not rendered lovable thereby.
> The murderer of Pepita
> looks at the Law unlovably. (*World*, 403)

Pepita, of course, is the victim of Jamaican Edward, and it is
implied by the context that he is the victim of the law (or feels
that he is), which he looks at "unlovably."

Sometimes conditions in the black community produce murders with the curious elements of innocence and love. "The
Murder" presents a grim but not too unfamiliar picture of ne-
glected children and their fate. While their mother "gossipped
down the street," two babies play with fire and the younger,
Percy is killed when Brucie whimsically sets Percy's clothes afire.
The persona is an omniscient observer but identified with the
children. The mixture of the tone of innocence with the horror of
the deed heightens the irony in the poem. The tone of the poem
does not indicate that Brucie is guilty, and it is obvious that the
gossiping and later mourning mother is not really guilty of
murder—merely of neglect of a loved one. In "The Ballad of
the Light-eyed Little Girl" there is a similar mix of murder,
neglect, and love. Sally mournfully buries her pet pigeon,
"whom she had starved to death." Like the mother in the last
poem, she blames herself but knows that the "murder" was "not
for lack of love."

Murder is a too common phenomenon in the black community,
as are the manifestations of oppression which spawn murder. As
indicated in the poems above, Miss Brooks recognizes several
kinds of murder, but they seem to be associated with black
people trying somehow to rid themselves of the "mind-forged
manacles" which restrict their lives.

War is another of the manacles that results in physical death.
Miss Brooks touches on this aspect of physical death in "Gay
Chaps at the Bar" and "Piano after War." In the first of these
Miss Brooks presents the irony of mature and sophisticated men

who were so utterly unprepared to deal with death. None of their experiences had taught them to die or to accept the death of their friends. The imagery of depicting death as "lions in the air" connotes a stalking, awesome monster that makes babies of men. "Piano after War" also deals with the effects of involvement with death on men. The sudden memory of death cries of fallen comrades precludes enjoyment of an evening's entertainment.

II *The Funeral*

In addition to murder and war, Miss Brooks's use of the funeral or related subjects expresses still more reflections of death. In "The Funeral" she deals mainly with the effects of physical death on those who attend the funeral. It is ironic that deceit, dishonesty, and the "blindfold" are the means of consolations. Clichés, flowers, and other traditional niceties are used to help ease the "dainty horrors."

The refrain "nothing but a plain black boy" in "Of DeWitt Williams on His Way to Lincoln Cemetery" suggests that Williams is a representative black man. On his last drive through the neighborhood he loved, he passed a number of places of frivolous entertainment. Miss Brooks's subtle message seems to be that the things that keep plain black boys going are also what stop them.[5]

"The Rites for Cousin Vit" depicts a funeral scene in which it is envisioned that Cousin Vit returns to the bars and love-rooms she knew. The name "Vit" ironically is used to suggest life, but again one has to question the effect of the "life" she had led. The answer is that the "high life" had killed her as it had DeWitt Williams and countless others. "Old Relative" represents another poem using funerals to suggest death. But like the other funeral poems, there is something almost humorous about this treatment:

> She went in there to muse on being rid
> Of relative beneath the coffin lid.
> No one was by. She stuck her tongue out; slid. (*World*, 72)

Since Miss Brooks very seldom brings humor into her poetry, one guesses that it is used for ironic effect in these last three poems dealing with funerals.[6]

Other poems that deal with physical death are "The Mother,"

"Still Do I Keep My Look, My Identity . . . ," "Southeast Corner," and "When I Die." The poem "The Mother" mourns the loss from aborted births—a not uncommon kind of death among blacks (*R*, 184). It could also remind us of the sadness of things that do not reach their potential, like a people whose natural growth and development has been stopped or changed. The sharp contrast between what could have been and what is sets off a mild dialectic of dreams versus reality. In the mother's imagination these babies still exist and grow, function, and die even while she knows they are dead. "Since anyhow you are dead" is the final resignation to reality as the mother returns from the fantasy she had drifted into. "Still Do I Keep My Look, My Identity . . ." shows the need of one who has pondered death to feel that there is an existence after death. The persona seems to seize this small island of consolation. In terms of the black man, a consolation for spiritual death is the retention of his physical look as well as his cultural identity. This effort for continuation after death is also depicted in "Southeast Corner." The name "Madam" implies a grandeur, while "underground" denotes death. The "fortune" spent on her funeral and burial suggests that a life-style of fineness is ironically continued in death:

> Her own grave is early found
> Where the thickest tallest monument
> Cuts grandly into the air. (*World*, 7)

The continuation has yet another irony, for one can easily infer that Madam was already "dead" while physically alive if she was primarily concerned with exhibition of material grandeur. "When I die" presents a striking contrast in the treatment after death. Little notice will be taken of the funeral except by an obviously poor husband or lover. Yet as in the last two poems, the dead's fortune will continue as in life. The man's shabby dress and his "buck-a-dozen" indicate that the woman feels she will continue in death to be "favored" with the shabbiness she experienced in life. She knows she will soon be forgotten.

III   *The Genesis of Spiritual Death*

The poems examined thus far have dealt with various kinds of expressions of physical death in the poetry of Gwendolyn Brooks. As stated earlier, most of these expressions go beyond a simple description of physical death to suggest the existence of a spiritual death as well. Indeed the spiritual death comprises the great bulk of Miss Brooks's treatment of death. As with physical death, the treatment of spiritual death can be separated into several distinct categories of poems including the genesis of spiritual death, deferred dreams, impotence and inferiority, resignation, high life, and other diversions.

The white man's basic way of thinking of the black man is one of the most powerful influences in the black man's environment, for it determines the way he treats the black man. Historically his way of thinking has created the conditions which cause physical and spiritual death in the black community. Therefore, those poems that reveal the white man's reactions to the black man will be used to describe the genesis of the spiritual death in Miss Brooks's poetry. It is important to note that many of these poems describe conditions that prevail from a decade up to even three decades ago.

In "A Bronzeville Mother Loiters in Mississippi. Meanwhile, a Mississippi Mother Burns Bacon," the emphasis appropriately is not on the murdered boy (who was not widely known before his death) but on the murderers and their kind. The poem deals with the story of the lynch-murder of Emmett Till, a fourteen-year-old Chicago black who was visiting relatives in Mississippi and allegedly made improper advances toward a white woman (the mock heroine of this poem). Presented from the point of view of the heroine, it reveals the genesis of preconditions of the physical and spiritual death of blacks—the moral perversions of whites who make up much of the debilitating environment of blacks. This is an important poem, for it epitomizes and dramatizes the fantastic unreality that prevails in the white man's concept of and dealings with the black man. The significant role of the pretext of protecting the white woman from black inhumanity makes this poem's theme central in dealing with the relation of whites to blacks.

The motif used is that of the mock ballad utilizing the hero, the heroine, and the villain. But it departs from the ballad form just as the conceptual framework of the hero and heroine departs from reality. The tone of the persona is sarcastic and sometimes presents the thoughts of the heroine and the actions of the fine prince in such a manner as to reveal their depravity. It is extremely ironic, for instance, that this obviously worldly and guilty woman wants or needs to think of herself as "the milk-white maid," the damsel in distress who was saved from a "dark villain" by her "fine prince." The "heroine" is obviously not comfortable with what she and her husband have done. She is shown to decline slowly from a position of idyllic romantic fantasy about her world:

> Herself: the milk-white maid, the "maid mild"
> of the ballad, Pursued
> By the Dark Villain, Rescued by the Fine Prince.
> The Happiness-Ever-After.
> That was worth anything.
> It was good to be a "maid mild."
> That made the breath go fast

—to disintegration:

> The one thing in the world that she did know and knew
> With terrifying clarity was that her composition
> Had disintegrated. That, although the pattern prevailed,
> The breaks were everywhere. That she could think
> Of no thread capable of the necessary
> Sew-work.

The description of the "dark villain" as an innocent child provides further irony:

> . . . the Dark Villain was a blackish child
> Of fourteen, with eyes still too young to be dirty,
> And a mouth still too young to have lost every reminder
> Of its infant softness.

The absurdity of the labels of "fine prince," "milk-white maid," and "dark villain" dramatizes the sham that is central to much of life in the United States which is governed by a philosophy that among other things perceives whites as desirable, enlightened, and vulnerable and blacks as despicable, depraved, and menacing.

The eyes of the Mississippi mother and her husband had been opened by the deed, "they knew both good and evil," and they were no longer innocent no matter how hard they tried. The perverted sense of justice in the poem dies with the physical death of Till and in its place comes a new sense of justice that forces itself on the heroine and hero in spite of their efforts to remain blind to it. This new sense of justice and in general broader perspective emanates from the human spirit and is therefore not only "big,/Bigger than all magnolias," and "spreading . . . over all of Earth and Mars," but it is also irresistible. The reference to being bigger than all magnolias suggests that the sense of their guilt and despicableness goes beyond the age-old customs of the South that condone and even reward such dastardly behavior. The "terrifying clarity" with which she sees her disintegration contrasts with the sense of confusion about a life-style and set of values foisted on her by the South. The characteristics of the ballad represent these values: ". . . she had never quite/Understood—the ballads they had set her to, in school." "Earth and Mars" suggests that the farthest reaches of her world and being have been colored by this act which she and her husband committed. Her "hatred for him burst into glorious flower: in spite of the effort to resist it:

> She tried, but could not resist the idea
> That a red ooze was seeping, spreading darkly, thickly, slowly,
> Over her white shoulder, her own shoulders . . .
> . . . .
> The courtroom beer and hate and sweat and drone,
> Pushed like a wall against her. She wanted to bear it.
> But his mouth would not go away and neither would the
> Decapitated exclamation points in the Other Woman's
> eyes.

The point is that, in spite of all, they desperately needed to appear desirable to each other as a means of justifying the act:

> He whispered something to her, did the Fine Prince.
> something
> About love, something about love and night and
> intention
> . . . .
> Whatever she might feel or half-feel, the lipstick
> necessity
> was something apart. He must never conclude
> That she had not been worth it. (*World*, 317–23)

The last quatrain is about the fear and hatred that she has for herself and her husband and the guilt that she must share with him.

In "Bronzeville Woman in a Red Hat," Miss Brooks again presents the poem through the eyes of a white woman who feels that she is wronged by the proximity of a black person. Again also it is clear that the tone of the poem is sympathetic toward the black woman and unsympathetic toward the white woman. Presenting the poem through the eyes of the ignorant and prejudiced white woman heightens the effect of the absurdity of her beliefs and gives the reader firsthand insight into the mentality that spawns an environment of death for black people because it perceives the presence of blacks as a threat to white purity. Mrs. Miles renders herself inhumane to the reader by the immediate irrational judgments she makes about the black woman. The imagery of the first six lines clearly indicates Mrs. Miles's prejudices. The black woman is referred to as "one" and evokes images of an attacking beast. "They had never had one in the house before." Somehow presence itself is a transgression —a strange loss of virginity. Her household, white and pure, was vulnerable to the menacing animal that had entered:

> The strangeness of it all. Like unleashing
> A lion, really, Poised
> To pounce. A puma, A panther, A black
> Bear.
> There it stood in the door.

Patsy Houlihan, the Irishwoman whom the black woman replaced, summarizes the qualities of Mrs. Miles as "Inhuman," a "fool," and a "cool one." Mrs. Miles remembers Patsy with smiles and had begged her to stay. When the "creamy child" was kissed by the black maid, Mrs. Miles's concept of the world was shattered very much as the Mississippi mother's world had been shattered: "World yelled, world writhed, world turned to light and rolled/Into her kitchen, nearly knocked her down." Perhaps the drastic fears and shocks brought about by something as innocuous as a woman kissing a baby reveal why the Mrs. Mileses of the world would find it necessary to safeguard the virgin purity of their homes and families by seeing to it that black people are kept in their places at all cost (R, 185):

> She, quite supposing purity despoiled,
> Committed to sourness, disordered, soiled,
> Went in to pry the ordure from the cream. (*World*, 351–54)

"The Lovers of the Poor" reveals another aspect of white mentality which results in spiritual death for blacks. The shifting point of view is again mainly that of the whites in the poems, and again the tone of the poem is consistently unfavorable toward the whites.[7] The members of the Ladies' Betterment League who have come to a slum tenement to give money to the poor are ultimately revealed as the worst kind of bigots, only slightly different from the Mississippi Mother and Mrs. Miles. The persona's bias is apparent when the positive qualities of the ladies are countered with negative ones which undermine them. For instance, they were said to have "proud, seamed faces with mercy and murder hinting." They have come with such narrowly conceived pictures of what the poor should be that, when the poor do not oblige them, they are offended. The sights, sounds, smells, decay are "entirely too much for them." Their league is allotting what the persona ironically terms "loathe love largess" to the lost, but they think their beautiful money will be wasted on such squalor. Their extreme insensitivity to the needs of the poor and the totally unrealistic approach to the betterment of the poor is evinced by the revulsion which the poor arouses in them and the haste with which the ladies flee to the safety and comfort of their own plush surroundings.

Another insight into the psyche of whites during the 1950s is afforded by "The Chicago Defender Sends a Man to Little Rock." The point of view is that of a reporter assigned to Little Rock during the height of its turmoil over public school desegregation to ascertain the nature of the people who lived there. The tone objectively describes them as "like people everywhere." This statement is not so much a defense of people in Little Rock as it is an indictment of white people in general who go about their daily routines hardly noticing the black man is there. Once blacks dare disturb the calm, however, whites—even in Little Rock—exercise the perversion of morality which to them justifies the atrocities done to blacks: "And true, they are hurling spittle, rock/Garbage and fruit in Little Rock" (*World*, 332). Obviously, the acts that Miss Brooks describes are not considered characteristic of the people of Little Rock. Yet the incongruities of "coiling storm awrithe" and "bright madonnas" and "a scythe of men harassing brown girls" suggest that people everywhere are capable of the same kinds of atrocities if the prevailing order is disturbed. Reference to the lynching of Jesus has the effect of universalizing this point. The tendency for blacks to recognize and respect the potential for violent atrocities by whites to keep blacks in their place spells another dimension of spiritual death in the black community.

Another poem which shows the genesis of the spiritual death among blacks is "Negro Hero." It provides a look at another aspect of the organized opposition to the advancement of black people toward fulfilling their concept of manhood. Having to break the white man's law in order to save him, the hero ironically points out that he was fighting the white man more than he was fighting the enemy. Realizing that the whites may not appreciate what he did and that the democracy for which he fought had a hidden knife waiting for him, the hero took his physical life into his hands and served them both.

The several pictures above of the genesis of spiritual death make obvious that it can lurk in many unsuspecting places and can exist side by side with ostensibly incongruous values. Since the problem of race in this country stems largely from the prejudiced attitudes of whites toward blacks, the poems expressing these attitudes are important in a discussion of the genesis of spiritual death in Miss Brooks's poetry.

IV Dreams Deferred

Deferred or canceled dreams comprise another aspect of spiritual death of Miss Brooks's poetry. Excellent examples of such a deprivation of dreams and the abundance of images that suggest a definite lack of life are found in "Kitchenette Building," where the environment itself precludes the survival of any dreams. "Things" in the first line connotes inanimate objects, pawns. "Dry hours" connotes drabness or emptiness that would stifle the human spirit. "Involuntary plan," like incidental genocide, is "excusable" or "invisible" because it can be fulfilled even if very few work to fulfill it. "Grayed in, and gray" is one of her many meaning-laden, but simple-sounding phrases. "Grayed in" refers again to the depressing and delimiting physical and psychological environment. The passive form of the verb confirms that blacks are acted upon as pawns whose environment is determined for them; hence, "and gray" is the result of being grayed in. The strong, awful necessities of life—ironically a common preoccupation of the weakest people—make "dream" a silly, out-of-place concept. The dialecticism of the dreams versus the overpowering presence of the most mundane aspects of life begins. The first two sentences of the poem set the stage for the contrast which is continued in the second stanza:

> But could a dream send up through onion fumes
> Its white and violet, fight with fried potatoes
> And yesterday's garbage ripening in the hall,
> Flutter or sing an aria down these rooms.

It is implied that the daily press of the mundane physical environment would stifle the delicate dream. The third stanza pits the dream against the psychological or spiritual environment:

> Even if we were willing to let it in.
> Had time to warm it, keep it very clean,
> Anticipate a message, let it begin? (*World*, 4)

In this poem we see a good example of Miss Brooks's use of dialectics to bring out the theme of spiritual death. She holds up the depressing setting and the characters that operate in it on the one hand and a dream on the other. She suggests the contrast, the "fight," the dream would have with the stultifying setting and with the brutalized characters.[8]

Miss Brooks, in "Hunchback Girl: She Thinks of Heaven," shows a contemplation of life after hell. The point of view is that of someone made to feel extremely depraved because of her appearance. The image of the hunchback is superb, for it is the epitome of deformity and ugliness. This suggests a woman who feels spurned and repulsive and longs for a different standard by which to be judged. A self-esteem low enough to make death preferable to life is indicative of spiritual death.

Again it is only after hell that the deferred dreams may be realized in "My Dreams, My Works, Must Wait Till after Hell":

> I hold my honey and I store my bread
> In little jars and cabinets of my will.

> I label clearly, and each latch and lid
> I bid, Be firm till I return from hell. (*World*, 50)

This poem may apply "hell" to war or to the black condition. War, like racism, is a monster that kills the human spirit and makes machines or shells of men. The ambiguity does not diminish the fact that the present condition is spiritual death or hell and only "when the devil days of . . . hurt drag out their last dregs" will spiritual life be possible.

In "The Anniad" the dreams are not deferred. If anything, they are premature. But when they are allowed to blossom, they are crushed. Annie dreams of her "paladin" and gets him. When he goes to war, Annie has to defer fulfillment of her dream until he returns. After returning, her lover finds her too tame for him. He "gets a maple [light-skinned] banshee . . . a sleek slit-eyed gypsy moan." After trying a number of diversions that do not last, Annie becomes a whore and thus is driven to her spiritual death by the relentless elimination of alternatives. The absence of the freedom and environment conducive to dreaming and fulfilling dreams deprives man of an essential quality of spiritual life.

V   *The Feeling of Powerlessness*

A number of Miss Brooks's poems deal with the absence of a sense of power or worth and seem to indicate that the lack of these qualities also contributes to the spiritual death in the black community.[9] " 'Pygmies Are Pygmies Still, Though Percht on Alps,' " for example, certainly deals with the subject of impotence and possibly is a sad poem about European strength and African weakness. The image of the "bleat" suggests an animal that is preyed upon or a beast of burden at best. The "Alps" place of the setting in Europe where pygmies "expand in cold impossible air." The image of someone pounding his breast-bone punily is an ironic one. Pounding the breast-bone is supposed to be a sign of power. Yet the giant "reaches no Alps: or knows no Alps to reach."

"Beverly Hills, Chicago" depicts this powerlessness by approaching the subject of the ghetto structures only indirectly in comparison to the white neighborhood. The blacks who are driving through the white neighborhood see everything there as superior to things in their own neighborhood: "Even the leaves fall down in lovelier patterns here." The whites seem so much more fortunate than the blacks that Nature smiles even on their leaves. This same feeling of inferiority is seen in another poem, "Strong Men, Riding Horses." Like the black people in "Beverly Hills, Chicago," Lester sees the whites as vastly superior to him. The expanse of their range ("from dawn to sunset") is a first clue to his awe before these "desert-eyed" heroes. This imagery along with "rentless" contrasts Lester's self-image with his image of the cowboys. The effect of the contrast between Lester and the cowboys is sharpened by the poem's being presented from Lester's point of view. This allows the poet to overstate or distort reality in order to focus attention on ironies in the overall situation. He thinks himself a coward, for paying rent in his own environment is implied to be a sign of impotence.

> What mannerisms I present, employ,
> Are camouflage, and what my mouths remark
> To word-wall off that broadness of the dark
> Is pitiful.
> I am not brave at all. (*World*, 313)

He thinks of his shams as phony efforts to look courageous and carefree. It is ironic that he sees the cowboys (who are really phony and "pasted to stars") as brave, while his own dealings with an actually dangerous environment are considered phony.[10] In a related poem, "We Real Cool," Miss Brooks is able to show the follow-up to the Lester mentality. By employing a diction of monosyllables and presenting the poem from the point of view of the young black men in the pool hall—a structure with its own mentality—the poem artfully allows tone to again reveal the ironies of the situation. The statement "We real cool" is partly the kind of mannerism that Lester had called camouflage. But an irony exists in the glaring fact that the monosyllabic talk hints at an aborted mental growth. Beyond this is the obvious fact that they are not "cool" at all but pitiable (like the giants wallowing on the plain.)[11] A more straightforward statement would be, "We are proficient at pool and high life as an escape from life competing with whites." They exemplify the "live-fast die-young pattern of many urban black youths." [12] They know ultimately that their diversions lead to death.

VI   *"The Sundays of Satin-Legs Smith"*

A longer poem devoted to a portrait of a ghetto man as he
attempts through highlife and other diversions to cope with
impotence and inferiority, "The Sundays of Satin-Legs Smith"
looms as one of the poet's most complete treatments of spiritual
death in the black community. For this reason it will be analyzed
here in terms of its statement on spiritual death as a whole
rather than in terms of its statements on impotence, inferiority,
high life, or other components of spiritual death individually.

Throughout the poem a sarcastic tone helps the reader to
recognize ironies as they occur.[13] Satin-Legs Smith's ego is
buoyed by the finest clothes and by doting women. He has rejected his shabby, common past and has convinced himself that
it is royal and fine. He even has streamlined his most common
name, "Smith," with "Satin-Legs." Everything he does is for the
aggrandizement of his self-esteem. He works at being blithely
oblivious of the true perspective of the world around him as
ironically hinted by "in a clear delirium." Only when he goes
to bed does he face the haunts of his past and the reality of who
and what he is. Hence, "he sheds with his pajamas, shabby days."
His resentments and fears go to bed with him.[14]

His ostentatious "need" for scent will not abide flowers, for
they remind him of death. At times the "plain black boy" image
seems to want to force its ways to the surface as the persona
informs the reader of a seamier side of Satin-Legs's life than the
one he displays:

> . . . cabbage and pigtails,
> Old intimacy with alleys, garbage pails,
> Down in the deep (But always beautiful) South
> Where roses blush their blithest (it is said)
> And sweet magnolias put Chanel to shame.

With this information one can easily understand why flowers
make him think of death. They remind him of his past—of his
real self. The poet helps evoke the thought of death in association
with the flowers by employment of death imagery to describe
the flowers which are "white," "cold," "formal," and "of . . .
straight tradition." So he uses "lotion, lavender, and oil" to make
his life "aromatic" yet safe from deathly associations.

With "the innards of his closet" the poet's deft imagery reveals a more intimate aspect of Satin-Legs. The "innards" (or entrails) suggest how visceral "his meticulous and serious love" —for self-image—is, and we simultaneously revisit the seamier chitterlings, pigtails, and other guts. More imagery with the description of the clothes reflects facets of Satin-Legs's personality. He is sarcastic and cocky when he wears his "wonder suits," but "scheduled to choke precisely" hints at an attached danger. "Hysterical" and "narrow banners for some gathering war" help bear this hint out. It becomes obvious that he is fighting for his "life" with the only weapons he has. The next two lines sum up Satin-Legs's desperate struggle with death for life.

> People are so in need, in need of help.
> People want so much that they do not know.

He is not really aware of what he needs so much. Now the irony of the "clear delirium" becomes even more apparent.

Below or beneath the buying of "things" is a great impulse to be a man that must be held in check because it is "impossible to show or spend." Like Matthew Cole, he must always smile and slide by life. The "promise piled over and betrayed" is a promise to himself to be a man. Long since he has betrayed that promise rather than risk or undertake to fulfill himself. Now, spiritually dead, he is subconsciously resigned to his impotence. What he fights is awareness of his impotence. The clothes pamper and love him and make him feel brave and beautiful, neat, graceful, accomplished.

He himself in his clothes is his own work of art. Other kinds of art are rejected because of their associations. As before when flowers were suggested, these things of "straight tradition" remind him of death. "Marble, complicated stone" becomes tombstones and morgue slabs, perhaps. Baroque, rococo, may become grotesque and deathly, causing him to "think with horror" of them. The persona again reminds the reader of Satin-Legs's background, to which all this "straight tradition" is alien and repulsive not only because of its macabre associations, but because it reminds him, by contrast, of his own impotence and death.

The tone turns decidedly negative as Satin-Legs is pictured

moving through his environment. "High life and distress" is used
here to suggest that life is born out of distress and leads to death.
Bought kisses and bought beer are spat out and spilled. The
sounds of the setting are described in negative terms: the
"meddling" alarm clock, the "governed" happiness of children,
"the dry tone of a plane," "oath," "consumption's spiritless ex-
pectoration," "indignant robin's resolute donation/Pinching a
track through apathy and din," "vendors weeping," and the
"horrible thought" of the L.

The pictures, too, are negative: "broken windows," "wornness,"
"patch," and the look of "Foodlessness." Satin-Legs listens to the
vendors singing the blues, and the persona again points out that
Satin-Legs could not like the classical musicians or accept the
"straight tradition" because his early basic experiences did not
prepare him to appreciate it. This man is a creature of his ancestors:

> The pasts of his ancestors lean against
> Him. Crowd him. Fog out his identity.
> Hundreds of hungers mingle with his own,
> Hundreds of voices advise so dexterously
> He quite considers his reactions his,
> Judges he walks most powerfully alone,
> That everything is—simply what it is.

This is an excellent statement of the influence of the total black
experience on Satin-Legs. The irony of Satin-Legs's activity is
revealed when the "great lover" is so impotent that he cannot
enjoy looking at the white heroine at the movies. His enjoyment
of Mickey Mouse is a subtle reference to his own mouselike
qualities. The innocuous frivolity of Mickey Mouse is reserved
for our regal peacock.

The poet's tone and diction once again so concentrate the
irony that the line "Squires his lady to dinner at Joe's Eats"
becomes a small summary to the whole poem. Although the term
"squires" can be taken to mean simply "escorts," it ironically
connotes escorting in a grand, dignified manner which for Satin-
Legs is an affectation designed to mollify his indignation and
camouflage his weakness. "His" is appropriate only if one thinks
of joint ownership, for he has a different "lady" every Sunday.
For all this finery to end up at Joe's Eats, which connotes the

greasy spoon, is more than a little humorous and more than a little sad: "You go out full./(The end is—isn't it?—all that really matters.)" The meal at Joe's Eats is like Satin-Legs's life: how much he lives is more vital than how well he lives. His quality of life being largely determined for him by his environment, he simply gets full. "And even and intrepid come/The tender boots of night to home." The poet here uses the term "intrepid" as she often uses "brave"—to suggest the high life, especially prostitution. For Satin-Legs Smith life is reduced to the sensual level, and any slip beyond brings horror and repulsion. The last six lines of the poem synopsize this dependence on the sensual to the exclusion of the spiritual:

> *Her body is like new brown bread*
> *Under the Woolworth mignonette.*
> *Her body is a honey bowl*
> *Whose waiting honey is deep and hot.*
> *Her body is like summer earth.*
> *Receptive, soft, and absolute. . . . (World, 26–31)*

"New brown bread" and "honey bowl" allude to his exclusively sensuous appetite. The term "Her body," which appears three times in the six lines, ambiguously refers to his sustenance and sexual pleasure, while more subtly suggesting death. This interpretation is consistent with the ambiguity of the grave-planting imagery, "like summer earth, receptive, soft, and absolute." The grave image suggests spiritual death in life and the planting image conversely refers to a hope of eventual spiritual rebirth from death.[15]

VII *High Life*

"The Sundays of Satin-Legs Smith" is a pivotal poem, linking Miss Brooks's treatment of impotence and high life, which is the next category of spiritual death to be considered. High life includes mainly activities related to prostitution, but also drinking, gambling, and other acts of frivolity which help one escape facing reality. A contemplation of the merits of high life is the subject of "A Song in the Front Yard," which presents a confrontation of classes with "back yard" folks depicted more favorably than "good" folks of the "front yard." "Charity chil-

dren" is an obvious reference to the poor class of people. "A girl
gets sick of a rose" expresses the same kind of rejection of in-
congruity that is found in "Kitchenette Building," where the
dream is so much out of place. There is a common longing to be
tangled up in the badness that apparently leads to trouble and
death. The poem is a quiet wish to enlist in that ambiguous army
of blacks and oppressed people who sometimes can only fight by
being "bad." Rejecting the "good" things of the oppressor makes
them bad and accepting the bad things makes them good. Roses
become bad and weeds become good, in this instance.

> But I say it's fine. Honest, I do.
> And I'd like to be a bad woman, too.
> And wear the brave stockings of night-black lace
> And strut down the streets with paint on my face. (*World*, 12)

Miss Brooks presents a positive picture of high life, especially
prostitution, through the eyes of a girl. The girl's use of the
word "brave" in talking of prostitution indicates that she knows
that her activities would lead to spiritual death. But she is tired
of being a good girl with no one to play with. So her alternatives
are to wither away in the stifling emptiness of the front yard or
live dangerously but fully in the back yard. In short, her choice
is between high life and no life.

"Sadie and Maud" is concerned with the same dialectic between the high life and no life. It is carried further, and we can
see the results of both. It is an important question, for many girls
in the black community are faced with this identical dilemma.
The tone of the poem is clearly more favorable toward Sadie
than Maud. One pities Maud, "a thin brown mouse," "all alone
in this old house." Her spiritual death is one of the impotence
and loneliness, while Sadie, "one of the livingest chits in all the
land," had "scraped life with a fine-toothed comb." The euphe-
mistic description of Sadie's death, "when Sadie said her last
so-long," is even less harshly put than Maud's reaction to Sadie's
two illegitimate babies. "Every one but Sadie nearly died of
shame." This reaction indicates Maud's restriction and control
by the rules of the front yard.

The title of "Obituary for a Living Lady" refers to the spiritual
death of the young woman who has spurned life for "God
country." As in "A Song in the Front Yard" and "Sadie and Maud"

a tone of disdain for the puritan standards of morality is evident.
They are presented as the shackles that bind and kill. The
dialectic in this poem between the high life and no life results
in the friend's choosing no life while the persona would obviously
have chosen the other.

Another example of high life as an escape from the death of
no life is Mary in "Gang Girls." The imagery of "a rose in a
whiskey glass" suggests that she can see beyond her own small
world but must operate within it. She resignedly admits that
"love's another departure," but she wonders if there will ever be
something more fulfilling in her life. The answer is that Mary
pays the price of nonloneliness, for escaping the no life, for she
is "terribly dying, under the philanthropy of robins."

"Do Not Be Afraid of No" also discusses the dilemma of a
young girl's choice between high life and no life. The tone of the
poem is opposite to that in the other poems dealing with this
problem. A reproving persona cautions against rushing into the
high life for material gains or to avoid the pain of loneliness. The
imagery continually equates the high life with death:

> Stupid, like a street
> That beats into a dead end and dies there, with nothing
>   left to reprimand or meet.

With deft imagery the poet describes the impotence of the high
life to make one forget his dismay:

> And like a candle fixed
> Against dismay and countershine or mixed
> Wild moon and sun

and the helplessness of a girl among skilled predators:

> and like
> A flying furniture, or bird with lattice wing; or gaunt thing,
>   a-stammer down a nightmare neon peopled with
>   condor, hawk and shrike.

This indirect statement she explains:

> To say yes is to die
> A lot or a little. The dead wear capably their wry
> Enameled emblems. They Smell. (*World*, 76–77)

The use again of the term "brave" for high life admits a grudg-
ing, limited respect for those who say yes. Ultimately reality
wins here as the addressee in the poem is persuaded to come
down to earth and avoid escape into death.

VIII   *Other Diversions*

Although "In the Mecca" contains numerous examples of
diversion of one kind or another, including high life, religion, art,
politics, and other preoccupations, the poem seems to view these
various preoccupations as gropings for truth and reality rather
than attempts to escape reality. Therefore, a detailed treatment
of this major poem will be reserved until Chapter 5.

A diversion quite apart from the high life is dealt with in "On
the Occasion of the Open-air Formation of the Olde Tymers'
Walking and Nature Club." The club is making a desperation
attempt to recapture something of the carefree, gay spirit of
youth by frolicking among nature's flowers and sunshine. The
possibility of failure to find happiness is frightening, for failure
would mean that they would have to turn and face death. The
diversion would be away from the awful presence of death.

The old-timers are trying to ward off the depression and eventual resignation that often accompany the nearness of physical
death. In some of Miss Brooks's poems resignation to one's physical or social prostration is evident as a subtheme. In "The Sonnet-
ballad" the tone is on the verge of resignation but still inclined
to desperation. The girl is sure that her lover who has gone to war
will not come back because he "would have to court Coquettish
death." "Looking," another poem about the effects of the war,
argues that any words to a departing soldier are really inappropriate and futile since nothing said or done can keep him from
harm.

"Matthew Cole" depicts a dispirited old man. Never smiling,
always sad, Cole waits for death with only memories to warm his
cold existence. He does not encounter life any more than necessary. He sits in his room and does not complain about the
roaches, heat, dust, rent, radio, and he smiles when he pays the
rent. The old-marrieds don't even talk because they are out of
tune with all the perfect preconditions of love. They just lie in
the darkness and wait.

"The Bean Eaters" presents a picture of two old people who

are waiting casually for death. The drabness and impotence suggested by the bean diet and such terms as "yellow," "plain," and "creaking" augment the hint of resignation. They have lived their day but keep hanging on, perfunctorily "putting on their clothes and putting things away." "Rented" connotes impotence, as does "back room." Like Matthew Cole, they relish their memories.

Another victim of spiritual death observed in Miss Brooks's poetry is the rejected or lonesome black woman. This sad figure has already been implied in "Hunchback Girl: She Thinks of Heaven," "The Anniad," and "The Ballad of Pearl May Lee." "Queen of the Blues" is a blues poem, however, that deals specifically with the loneliness of a black woman. It presents a "blues" within a blues: both the story about Mame and the story she tells are blues of loneliness. Bereft of her family and more lately her "daddy," she is momentarily consoled by the M.C.'s reference to her as "queen of the blues." The irony of the situation is that men, who pinch her arms and slap her thighs, do not respect her. The thought is painful to Mame, who thinks men are "low down dirty and mean" for not tipping their hats to a queen. Mabbie's thoughts also are painful in "The Ballad of Chocolate Mabbie," a poem of rejection because of color. Willie Boone, whom Mabbie loved, preferred lighter-skinned girls. Mabbie's sad, abrupt encounter with this fact causes her thoughts to turn inward, possibly transferring to a self-rejection the rejection she had experienced from Willie Boone.[16]

"When Mrs. Martin's Booker T" is concerned with a different kind of rejection. Mrs. Martin has her idea about what her neighbors think. It is clear that a disgraceful act of her son's is worse to her than her death would be. She moves to another part of town because she is ashamed of her son. She feels that he is already spiritually dead if he does not "take that gal and get her decent wed." In this short poem there are four references to some kind of death. Implicit in "Ruined Rosa Brown" is the old idea that she is no longer spiritually capable or worthy of living unless her situation is remedied by being "decent wed." "The end of my days" refers to Mrs. Martin's own physical death. Mrs. Martin feels that by being a disgrace, she too is spiritually dead and has slunk off "to the low west side of town" to wait for death. The spiritual aspect of Mrs. Martin's death at the time of the poem is evinced in the line "He wrung my heart like a chicken neck." He has killed her—the passage does not refer to a wounding but to a deliberate killing. This imagery is important, for it explains how she can be harsh with her son. "Don't come to tell me he's dying" and "Don't come to tell me he's dead" refer to physical death but are used here to show physical death's relative unimportance compared to spiritual death.

Mrs. Martin's despair, though sufficiently drastic for her to move to another part of town, is still less drastic than that felt by those in the black ghetto who feel driven to contemplate suicide. Arthur P. Davis sees Miss Brooks's poems that depict individuals considering suicide as "indications of spiritual bankruptcy" in the black ghetto.[17] A woman in "A Sunset of the City," faced with middle age, knows that winter is soon to follow the present fall. The empty drabness of her existence prompts her to consider: "is 'humming pallor' a better fate than death"? (*R*, 184). A related emptiness causes a similar question from the bewildered individual in "A Man of the Middle Class." While enjoying material success, he has sold his soul to the extent of bankruptcy, never takes a stand or even exposes himself, and therefore "appears to himself ineffectual." For answers he considers but rejects the solutions of those he has imitated—those shooting themselves and jumping out of windows (*R*, 186). Suicide is considered but rejected also in "The Contemplation of Suicide: The Temptation of Timothy." Here as in the other suicide poems the protagonist questions the worthwhileness of his existence:

> One poises, poses, at track, or range, or river,
> Saying, What is the fact of my life, to what do I tend?

Once again, however, death is rejected because there is still enough selfish curiosity about life:

> Too selfish to be nothing while beams break, surf's
> epileptic, chicken reeks or squalls. (*World*, 355)

A final category of poems on spiritual death deals with the burdens of the spiritually dead. In "Jessie Mitchell's Mother" the mother is an obvious burden to the daughter, who wishes her mother dead ("Only a habit would cry if she should die"). Jessie's responsibility is to serve as a nurse to her invalid mother who, according to Jessie, "is jelly-hearted and—has a brain of jelly." A girl expresses relief from a similar situation in "Old Relative" by secretly sticking out her tongue at the corpse who had died after the baths and bowel-work. Even the perfunctory week of mourning is excessive when "she must not play 'Charmaine,' or 'Honey Bunch,' or 'Singing in the Rain.'" In "Throwing Out the Flowers" the same kind of practical attitude is taken toward cleaning up after an elaborate Thanksgiving dinner. Once the meal is over, "the duck fats rot" and "the broccoli, yams and the bead-buttermilk are dead." The flowers are thrown out unceremoniously ("brusque burial") since, as with the other parts of the occasion, when their purpose or function is ended, they are dead. The vase breath represents the quality of life which is better after removal of the dead and stinking flowers. The old relative and Jessie Mitchell's mother, having both outlived any useful purpose, were burdens on the living. "Throwing out the flowers" helps emphasize the point that when people have outlived their useful functions and become burdens on the living, mourning after their death can often be perfunctory.

The substantial portion of Miss Brooks's poetry that deals with the theme of "spiritual death" includes a number of more easily recognizable subthemes such as war, murder, funerals, white prejudices, deferred dreams, impotence and inferiority, high life, resignation, and loneliness under one large heading. Anyone who perennially must defer his dreams, who feels impotent or inferior, who relies on frivolity to escape dealing with harsh realities, who is resigned to physical or psychological deprivation, or who is lonesome or rejected can be said to be dispirited or spiritually dead. Miss Brooks implies strongly that certain of these subthemes are tantamount to death.

All the despairing content of the poems discussed in this chapter notwithstanding, Miss Brooks's poetry as a whole is not fatalistic in its approach to the total black experience. As indicated earlier, the poet foresees brighter tomorrows for the black man and for the world. A significant role in achieving these brighter tomorrows is being played by the black man's sense of his past which guides him in shaping the future. The awareness of his past is in part the subject of the next chapter.

CHAPTER 4

The Fall from Glory

REGARDLESS of what portion of the collective memory of a person is fantasy and what portion is fact, the memory can play an important role in establishing the parameters of behavior for a people, shaping their life-styles, their adjustment to the physical and social environment, and ultimately their destinies.

This sense, whether it is referred to as intuitive knowledge, subconscious desires, instincts, or some other name, has influenced the black man's actions and subsequently his treatment from his earliest experience with Europeans and European-Americans. It is not surprising that the slave spirituals are replete with notions of "going home." While most poetry and art in general employ the wiles of indirection, black people have been forced to rely upon them as a matter of physical well-being to express their thoughts and innermost subconscious yearnings. Spirituals, slave rhymes, blues, jazz, and even everyday speech become for the black man indirect expressions and deferred dreams.[1]

This chapter is an attempt to show that the poetry of Gwendolyn Brooks deals substantially with the theme of the fall from glory. It contends that even though the black man's present condition is that of spiritual death, he inherits a strong racial sense of having fallen from a past glory and that this sense or memory, as evinced in Miss Brooks's poetry, is a pivotal factor in the black man's survival and his dreams of an eventual Phoenix-like rebirth from the ashes of his ruin. Since racial memory is an important part of the black man's sense of having fallen from glory, allusions to memory, especially to memories of conditions that are better than the present ones, collectively serve to develop the theme of the fall from glory. The allusions range from specific reference to the black man's remembering his freedom and power in Africa to vague suggestions of a remembrance of a situation better than the present. Similarly Miss Brooks uses references to home, returning, and Africa to evoke the idea of a lost glory. References to these terms are often made individually but are so closely related in the black experience that they sometimes appear in combinations of two or three. Because in her poetry Africa is home for the black man and because memories of home often compare favorably with appraisal of the present, allusions to returning seem to follow naturally. The favorable comparison which gives rise to the sense of having fallen from glory to ruin is symbolized by many other kinds of negative displacement evinced by the general movement of the situations in Miss Brooks's poems from good to bad.

As vivid memories of Africa faded and as expression of desire to return remained indirect, the black man looked to symbols that would express the thought and give some relief to a pent-up soul refused the right to fully cry. One convenient vehicle for such symbolic expression was the Christian religion. The whole idea of the triumph over oppression and a rebirth in glory allowed the black man to vent expression of his pent-up desires. Miss Brooks uses the Christian theme, but she also uses the War, unrequited love, and other common occurrences in black life to convey the theme of a fall from glory.

I   *Memory as Misery and Pleasure*

Miss Brooks shows in her poetry that memory can be a mixture of misery and pleasure when it is all that one has of a glory that is taken or otherwise gone. A notable number of her poems include situations dealing with the sense of negative displacement brought on by memory of a pleasant experience that no longer exists. Usually the tone betrays a hint of hope or optimism that the situation will get better, indeed that by hanging on or surviving, the rememberers hope to help restore that which is lost.

In "On the Occasion of the Open-Air Formation of the Olde Tymers' Walking and Nature Club" the "olde tymers" make a desperate attempt to recapture something of the carefree, gay spirit of youth by frolicking among nature's flowers and sunshine as depicted in these lines:

> We shall go playing in the woods again!

> The flowers and fruits and nuts and sun have waited.
> And when we come, we merry girls and men,
> They will unlock themselves, and be elated.
>
> And we shall walk among them, working well
> At this delicious business of being gay.
> And we shall push our laughter like a bell,
> Trying to make it ring in the old way.

These lines suggest that at least some happiness is gained simply by remembering things as they were "the old way." The next stanza, however, shows that the possibility of failure to find happiness is frightening, for then they will have to turn to face death:

> But if our romp is rusty, if we fumble,
> If we fall down, and if our festival
> Of molded mirth should crack, or even crumble,
> Have mercy, flowers! sun, forgive us all. (*World*, 356)

Implicit in these lines is that the romp or all such attempts to experience things that are gone will eventually cease to be successful diversions from the awful presence of death.

In some cases memory is all that people have left of former more favorable situations. In such cases they savor their memories as treasures and bring them out occasionally to fondle them or feast on them. Very often Miss Brooks depicts negative displacement in squalid or destitute surroundings. Matthew Cole, for example, is drawn as a character with only memories to cheer him. Cole's utterly joyless existence in his squalid, cold, and lonesome room is interrupted only by the "gloomy house-keeper/Who forgets to build the fire/And the red fat roaches that stroll/Unafraid up his wall. . . ."[2] Cole's only consolation as he sits in his hell and survives is the memories of his happier childhood:

> He never smiles. Except when come,
> Say, thoughts of a little boy licorice-full
> Without a nickel for Sunday School.
> Or thoughts of a little boy playing ball
> And swearing at sound of his mother's call.
> Once, I think, he laughed aloud,

> At thought of a wonderful joke he'd played
> On the whole crowd, the old crowd. . . . (*World*, 24)

Here "the old crowd" suggests a wistful longing for bygone days similarly to "the old way" in the previous poem. Unlike the "olde tymers" of the previous poem, however, he has no illusions about ever again enjoying actual pleasant experiences similar to those he enjoyed in the past. In both poems Miss Brooks used lock imagery to suggest the degrees of inaccessibility of the past. While the "old tymers" hope that the "flowers and fruits and nuts and sun . . . will unlock themselves," Cole sits in the "door-locked dirtiness of his room" with only his memories to cheer him. Although there is a painful sense of loss in the poems, Miss Brooks shows the healing efficacy of memories.

In "Jessie Mitchell's Mother," for instance, the mother's envy of Jessie for being young, thin, and straight in contrast to her own old "ballooning body" that was like a "stretched yellow rag" is evidenced in these lines: "Comparisons shattered her heart, ate at her bulwarks:/The shabby and the bright: she, almost hating her daughter. . . ." The mother, like many others who have undergone a negative displacement in the major aspects of their lives, relies on memories of happier days to sustain her. The account of her reflection on her youth and the subsequent effect illustrates the sustaining power of memory:

> Mine, in fact, because I was lovely, had flowers
> Tucked in the jerks, flowers were here and there. . .
> She revived for the moment settled and dried-up triumphs,
> Forced perfume into old petals, pulled up the droop.
> Refueled
> Triumphant long-exhaled breaths.
> Her exquisite yellow youth. . . . (*World*, 328) [3]

The "old yellow pair" in "The Bean Eaters" seem resigned to the drabness of everyday life, including their staple of beans:

> They eat beans mostly, this old yellow pair.
> Dinner is a casual affair.
> Plain chipware on a plain and creaking wood,
> Tin flatware.
>
> Two who are Mostly Good.

> Two who have lived their day,
> But keep on putting on their clothes
> And putting things away.

Having lived their day, they are putting things away as if winding down an operation and readying for withdrawal from activity. The word "but" used with "putting things away" also suggests a desire for neatness and order that represents a determination to keep on living, a refusal to give up and let things go. They are more nourished and sustained by their memories than by their beans:

> And remembering. . .
> Remembering, with twinklings and twinges,
> As they lean over the beans in their rented back
>   room that is full of beads and receipts and
>   dolls and cloths, tobacco crumbs, vases and
> fringes. (*World*, 314)

The poet juxtaposes the plainness and bareness of their rented back room with the "twinklings and twinges" that accompany the memories of better days mixed with pain and with the fullness of the mementos that surround them. They bought these trinkets and the attendant memories with their spent lives, and the receipts suggest the record of dues paid.

Memory supports not only the elderly in their trial with impending death but can also help anyone overcome trying situations. What sustains Emmett's mother in "The Last Quatrain of the Ballad of Emmett Till" is her memory of her son alive:

> Emmett's mother is a pretty-faced thing;
>   the tint of pulled taffy.
> She sits in a red room
>   drinking black coffee.
> She kisses her killed boy.
>   And she is sorry.
> Chaos in windy grays
>   through a red prairie. (*World*, 324)

In the maddening chaos around her she stabilizes herself and carries on by "kissing" "her killed boy." Of course, she can do this only through memory.

Memory involving negative displacement is not always pleasant, however, in the usual sense. Way-out Morgan, one of the characters who people the Mecca apartment building in "In the Mecca," savors memories of atrocities to black people:

> Way-out Morgan is collecting guns
> in a tiny fourth-floor room.
> He is not hungry, ever, though sinfully lean
> He flourishes, ever, on porridge or pat of bean
> pudding or wiener sour-fills fearsomely
> on visions of Death-to-the-Hordes-of-the-White-Men!
> Death!
>   (This is the Maxim painted in big black
>   above a bed bought at a Champlain rummage sale.)
> Remembering three local-and-legal beatings, he
> rubs his hands in glee,
> does Way-out Morgan. Remembering his Sister
> mob-raped in Mississippi, Way-out Morgan
> smacks his lips and adds another gun
> and listens to Blackness stern and blunt and beautiful,
> organ-rich Blackness telling a terrible story.
> Way-out Morgan
> predicts the Day of Debt-pay shall begin.
> the Day of Demon-diamond,
> of blood in mouths and body-mouths,
> of flesh-rip in the Forum of Justice at last!
> Remembering mates in the Mississippi River,
> mates with black bodies once majestic, Way-out
> postpones a yellow woman in his bed, postpones
> wetnesses and little cries and stomachings—
> to consider Ruin. (*World*, 400–401)

He is a bean eater of sorts. Never hungry, he eats perfunctorily—largely beans—and he is sustained not by the food he eats but by his vision and memories. As in "The Bean Eaters," the plainness of the physical surroundings and the meagerness of his meal sharply contrast the fearsome fullness and richness of his thoughts. Indeed the poet after describing the diet of "porridge or pat of bean pudding or wiener soup" goes on to describe his visions and memories in language that suggests eating. Hence he "fills fearsomely," "smacks sweet his lips," and predicts the day of "blood in mouths and body-mouths/of flesh-rip in the Forum of Justice at last!" The postponing of sex with the yellow woman in his secondhand bed and the bland, objective way sex is referred to further indicate a subjection of his physical wants to his preoccupation with retribution and ruin. "Ruin" in this poem refers to both the fall of the black man and Morgan's contemplation of destruction of the white man. Visions of the day of Debt-pay—not the atrocities themselves—and the idea that the blacks were "once majestic" underlie his glee and accentuate the feeling of loss in each incident in the "terrible story" that Blackness is telling.

II   *Protest as the Road to Recovery*

A significant aspect of the "terrible story" of the black man is the sense of returning to a vague healing condition where his burdens would be lifted and his lost glory regained. Sometimes the black man's protest of his ruin involves a sense of returning to a more favorable condition. In "People Protest in Sprawling Lightless Ways" the form of the protest implies a negative displacement from life to death. After indicating the variety of ways people protest against their deceivers short of "censures" and "damns," the poet presents the following pleading protest by "man crying up to any one—":

> Be my reviver; Be my influence,
> My reinstated stimulus, my loyal.
> Enable me to give my golds goldly.
> To win.
> To
> Take out a skulk, to put a fortitude in.
> Give me my life again, whose right is quite
> The charm of porcelain, the vigor of stone. (*World,* 122)

"Reviver" and "reinstated stimulus" and "give me my life again" indicate that the speaker's former condition is better than his present condition and that he wants to experience and possess what he had in the past. The present condition does not allow him to give his gold goldly, to win, or to displace fear with strength according to his right to beauty and strength. His sense of having fallen from a position of power causes him to "follow many a cloven foot" in an effort to return.

Sometimes the poet is less vague and refers to "going home" instead of simply "returning." Miss Brooks uses the idea of home in a way that suggests the black man's fall from power and beauty to impotence, ugliness, and death. "One Wants a Teller in a Time like This" deals with the idea that one cannot make the necessary correct decisions by himself. He needs a Teller to find the way home:

> One cannot walk this winding street with pride,
> Straight-shouldered, tranquil-eyed,
> Knowing one knows for sure the way back home.
> One wonders if one has a home.

The loss of the home itself, the way to it, and the certainty that it exists show the deteriorated condition of the black man as he gets farther from home. In "Of DeWitt Williams on His Way to Lincoln Cemetery" there is a sense of returning home evoked by part of the spiritual "Swing Low, Sweet Chariot" which suggests "coming for to carry me home." As he is driven for the last time past the places he frequented on Chicago's South Side, the chariot is carrying him away from the death of the high life described in the poem as the pool hall, the show, dance halls, "where he picked his women, where/He drank his liquid joy." He is going to a place more befitting to be home for a "plain black boy," as he is described at the beginning and near the end of the poem.[4]

Miss Brooks's use of the subject of war often objectifies the desire to return home. The experience of the soldier longing for home is similar to that of the embattled black man who dreams vaguely of home. A strong sense of returning to a happier state is expressed in "My Dreams, My Works, Must Wait till after Hell." It is clear that the persona is making preparation to return:

> I hold my honey and I store my bread
> In little jars and cabinets of my will.
> I label clearly, and each latch and lid
> I bid, Be firm till I return from hell.

Impatient with the hell he is in, he is advised only to wait. He hopes that when he remembers to go home, he will still be able to enjoy those things which he was free to enjoy before hell. Although the poem deals to some extent with a contemplation of the good life after hell, the actual movement that has taken place is from a condition of relative good to a hellish one. Miss

Brooks illustrates that hell is more spiritual than physical by focusing attention on the persona's concerned introspection:

> No man can give me any word but Wait,
> The puny light. I keep eyes pointed in;
> Hoping that, when the devil days of my hurt
> Drag out to their last dregs and I resume
> On such legs as are left me, in such heart
> As I can manage, remember to go home,
> My taste will not have turned insensitive
> To honey and bread old purity could love. (*World*, 50)

The implication is the "puny light" or promise that things will be better is not so important as the survival of the spirit which will make enjoyment of the good life possible, if it should return.

III   *The Memory of Africa*

Still more specifically Miss Brooks symbolizes the glory from which black people have fallen by references to Africa, the home remembered—if sometimes only vaguely—and to which spiritually blacks are rapidly returning. Her treatment of the sub-theme of a former African glory ranges from peripheral allusions to very direct statements. In "In the Mecca," for instance, the hints are rather indirect. The first allusion to Africa occurs as Mrs. Smith is climbing the steps in the Mecca. Hyena, the golden-haired whore, suggests Africa because the animal hyena is native to Africa. She also comes bursting forth ambiguously like a wild animal flushed from cover or like a predator suddenly striking from the place of hiding:

> Out of her dusty threshold burst Hyena
> The striking debutante, A fancier of firsts.
> One of the first, and to the tune of hate,
> In all the Mecca to paint her hair sun-gold.

Later in the poem when he is asked whether he has seen the little lost girl, Pepita, Alfred refers to Africa in favorable terms:

> No, Alfred has not seen Pepita Smith,
> But he (who might have been a poet-king)
> can speak superbly of the line of Leopold.

The line of Leopold is thick with blackness
   and Scriptural drops and rises.
The line of Leopold is busy with betrothals of royal
   rage and conditional pardon and with
refusal of mothballs for outmoded love.
Senghor will not shred
love,
gargantuan gardens careful in the sun,
fairy story gold, thrones, feast, the three princesses,
. . . .
                                          Alfred can tell of
Poet, and muller, and President of Senegal, who
in voice and body
loves sun,
listens
to the rich pound in and beneath the black feet of
   Africa. (*World*, 378, 391–93)

The point here is that Africa offers a rich heritage of which black
citizens of the United States have been bereft. References to
Senghor, Leopold, "negritude," and Senegal help to elicit the
image of Africa. The sense of loss is augmented by the idea expressed by Alfred that he "might have been an architect" or
"a poet-king" like Leopold Sedar Senghor, coiner of the term
"negritude." The beauty and power of the poetry of Senghor as
well as the beauty and power of his African freedom epitomize
African heritage, the loss of which Alfred and the black man in
general feel so deeply.[5]
   In "The Vacant Lot" the references are somewhat more central
to the thrust of the poem than they were in "In the Mecca." The
building's absence is a kind of negative displacement, as is the
absence of the family and their activities:

Mrs. Coley's three-flat brick
Isn't here any more.
All gone with seeing her fat little form
Burst out of the basement door'
And with seeing her African son-in-law
   (rightful heir to the throne)

With his great white strong cold squares of teeth
And his little eyes of stone'
And with seeing the squat fat daughter

> Letting in the men
> When majesty has gone for the day—
> And letting them out again.

The activities themselves also involve negative displacement. The African son-in-law with his retained sense of majesty ironically illuminates the depth to which this majesty has fallen by his wife's having to be a whore. Interestingly Miss Brooks uses very similar introductions to the whore, Hyena, in "In the Mecca": "Out of her dusty threshold burst Hyena" compared with "Burst out of the basement door" in "The Vacant Lot." Again the image is ambiguous—suggesting both a flushed quary and an attacking predator, an image Miss Brooks sometimes uses in referring to prostitutes.

"Old Laughter" affords an example of a very direct statement about Africa involved in negative displacement. The first two stanzas present an idyllic description of the land and its people:

> The men and women long ago
> In Africa, in Africa,
> Knew all there was of joy to know.
> In sunny Africa
> The spices flew from tree to tree.
> The spices trifled in the air
> That carelessly
> Fondled and twisted hair.
>
> The men and women richly sang
> In land of gold and green and red.
> The bells of merriment richly rang.

With an almost cruel abruptness, the poet then describes the fallen Africa:

> But richeness is long dead,
> Old laughter chilled, old music done
> In bright, bewildered Africa.
>
> The bamboo and the cinnamon
> Are sad in Africa.

To the extent that black people of the United States identify with Africa, the negative displacement is shared by them. The fall is from life to death, joy to sadness, singing to chilled laughter, merry bells to old music done.

IV *"Riders to the Blood-Red Wrath"*

Perhaps the most complete treatment of the theme of the fall from glory is found in "Riders to the Blood-Red Wrath." Set against a background of the freedom rides of the early 1960s, the poem includes a sense of racial memory of former glory, particularly in Africa, along with employment of every other dominant theme treated in this book. For now, however, the discussion will be limited to the sense of fall from glory. The persona seems to be speaking for the black man as he remembers Africa, and the black man's racial memory of Africa focuses on the most pleasant of aspects. First, the splendor of Africa is recalled:

> I remember kings.
> A blossoming palace. Silver, Ivory.
> The conventional wealth of stalking Africa.
> All bright, all Bestial. Snarling marvelously.

And second, the freedom the black man enjoyed in Africa:

> I remember my right to roughly run and roar.
> My right to raid the sun, consult the moon,
> Nod to my princesses or split them open,
> To flay my lions, eat blood with a spoon.
> You never saw such running and such roaring!—
> Nor heard a burgeoning heart to craze and pound!—
> Nor sprang to such a happy rape of heaven!
> Nor sanctioned such a Kinship with the ground!

The point here is that the black man "remembers" being able to do whatever he wanted in Africa. The poem implies that, to someone in utter thralldom, the memories of Africa are extremely important for his survival:[6]

> They do not se how deftly I endure.
> Deep down the whirlwind of good rage I store
> Commemorations in an utter thrall.
> Although I need not eat them any more.

It is only because these memories and "the whirlwind of good rage" are controlled "in an utter thrall" that the black man's survival is possible.

Next, the memory depicts part of the hellish experience of the fall. The scene aboard the slave ship represents an abrupt change from utter freedom to utter thralldom:

> And I remember blazing dementias
> Aboard such trade as maddens any man.
> . . . The mate and captain fragrantly reviewed
> The fragrant hold and presently began
> Their retching rampage among their luminous
> Black pudding, among the guttural chained slime;
> Half fainting from their love affair with fetors
> That pledged a haughty allegiance for all time.

Noteworthy is the poet's ploy of shifting the emphasis from the black man to his oppressor during and after the fall. The mate and the captain and their "fragrant" fetor rape of "their luminous black pudding" are but symbols of the larger rape of Africa by Europe and European America. The poet implies that the spiritual stench, which is a permanent part of the European, came from and comes from his "love affair with fetors"—that by dehumanizing he becomes dehumanized and by enslaving he becomes a slave.

Another scene alluded to from the fallen condition is that of the period of physical slavery in the United States:

> I recollect the latter lease and lash
> and labor that defiled the bone, that thinned
> My blood and blood-line. All my climate my
> Foster designers designed and disciplined. (SP, 115–18).[7]

Here the negative effects of the fall are mentioned. The black man in this stage of his experience is driven like a depraved animal weakening him and his blood-line. The extreme depth of the spiritual fall is obvious when one notices that before the fall the black man "sprang to such a happy rape of heaven" and after the fall the black man's whole environment is "designed and disciplined" by his "foster designer," the white man.

V *Negative Displacement*

Besides dealing with the fall from glory through examples of racial memories, a vague sense of vindication and returning to a long-lost home, and former African splendor and freedom, Miss Brooks's poems reflect the general direction of the black experience—from glory to ruin—with a predominance of movements from good to bad situations. Perhaps the least equivocal are those poems that depict a movement from physical life to physical death. For this reason there appears no need to do more than point out these poems. Negative displacement is evident in "Southeast Corner," "In the Mecca," "Malcolm X," "Medgar Evers," "The Ballad of Rudolph Reed," "The Ballad of Pearl May Lee," "A Bronzeville Mother Loiters in Mississippi. Meanwhile a Mississippi Mother Burns Bacon," "When I Die," and others. In each of these poems the sorrow attended by the death clearly indicated that life is considered preferable to death.

Movement from happiness to sorrow which is tantamount to spiritual death also appears frequently in Miss Brooks's poetry. Very often this movement involves a girl or woman going from euphoric rapture to spiritual mortification because of an unhappy experience with love. A rather clear case of movement of this kind is presented in "Obituary for a Living Lady." The title strongly suggests the theme of this poem. Here the structures of religion are equated to death, for they preclude the enjoyment of many of life's frivolous pleasures. The lovely young woman in the poem, seemingly with so much to live for, retreats into "death" after an unsuccessful love affair. A similar case of unrequited love is found in "The Ballad of Chocolate Mabbie." Mabbie is in heaven just being near Willie Boone or waiting for him outside the grammar-school gates. When one day he walks out with "a lemon-hued lynx" (a yellow-skinned girl), Mabbie is mortified "with hush in the heart."

In "The Anniad" the main theme is again the movement of a girl from innocence and optimistic ideals about love to spiritual ruin because of a shattering experience with love. In the beginning this girl dreams of a bold and handsome "paladin" who would be a composite of all the virtues and many other attractive characteristics a girl would want in a man. She finds him (man of tan), worships him, and is seduced by him. War takes him away for a while. When he returns he finds her too sweet and tame, for now, after his experiences abroad, he needs a woman wild and potent to help him regain his lost potency. When he rejects her and chooses a more worldly woman, the girl is crushed. She seeks solace in a number of diversions. Man of tan comes back spent and dying. She takes him in and cares for him. When he dies, she dies spiritually and becomes a prostitute, living only perfunctorily. From this synopsis it is evident that the action moves from good to bad. Miss Brooks helps the reader to focus on the fall from one extreme to the other by use of several similar passages, each describing a different milestone in the girl's movement from happiness to misery. She is first described in this way:

> Think of sweet and chocolate,
> Left to folly or to fate,
> Whom the higher gods forgot,
> Whom the lower gods berate;
> Physical and underfed
> Fancying on the featherbed
> What was never and is not.
> . . . .
> Think of ripe and rompabout,
> All her harvest buttoned in,
> All her ornaments untried;
> Waiting for the paladin
> Prosperous and ocean-eyed
> Who shall rub her secrets out
> And behold the hinted bride.

These passages summarize her innocence and her "ripeness" for love. When man of tan rejects her for another woman, she is described as being bereft of the pleasantries that make life worthwhile:

> Think of sweet and chocolate
> Minus passing-magistrate,
> Minus passing-lofty light,
> Minus passing-stars for night,
> Sirocco wafts and tra la la,
> Minus symbol, cinema
> Mirages, all things suave and bright.

Finally, she is left alone with only her prostitution and her memories:

> Think of tweaked and twenty-four.
> Fuchsias gone or gripped or gray,
> All hay-colored that was green,
> Soft aesthetic looted, lean,
> Crouching low, behind a screen,
> Pock-marked eye-light, and the sore
> Eaglets of old pride and prey.
> . . . .
> Think of almost thoroughly
> Derelict and dim and done.
> Stroking swallows form the sweat.
> Fingering faint violet.
> Hugging old and Sunday sun.
> Kissing in her kitchenette
> The minutes of memory. (*World*, 83, 93)

In the same way that Emmett Till's mother sits in a red room kissing her killed boy, the girl in this poem in her kitchenette is "kissing" her most pleasant memories while she dismisses unpleasant memories of his (man of tan's) kick and kiss.

The subtheme of a young woman passing from happiness to misery because of rejection by a lover is most succinctly yet completely expressed in "For Clarice It Is Terrible Because with This He takes Away All the Popular Songs and the Moonlights and Still Night Hushes and the Movies with Star-eyed Girls and Simpering Males." The not-so-succinct title alone provides a literal account of negative displacement, for all the experiences that formerly brought pleasure now bring sorrow. As with the other poems dealing with unhappy lovers, this poem begins with an expression of the great expectations of happiness to be derived from love: "They were going to have so much fun in the summer." This technique immediately positions the heroine for the fall she takes, which is more poignant if there is evidence of innocence and naive optimism. The title here suggests that the heroine is somewhat innocent and naive because of the frivolous nature of the experiences which she associates with love. The hurt generated from this rejection is anything but frivolous, however, as the harsh imagery in the first stanza reveals:

> But winter has come to the edges of his regard.
> Not the lace-ice, but the bleak, the bleak steep sorrow.
> Not the shy snow, not the impermanent icicles but the hard
> The cruel pack and snarl of the unloved cold.

The second stanza depicts her withdrawal, her sense of desperate
aloneness, and fear of "the desert death of tomorrow":

> There is nowhere for her to go.
> There is no tenderness on whom she may frankly cry.
> There is no way to unlatch her face
> And show the gray shudder
> Of this hurt hour
> And the desert death of tomorrow. (*World*, 348)

Another kind of negative displacement involves the movement
from youth to old age. As in the movement from life to death,
the resistance to movement from youth to old age indicates that
it is usually considered a negative direction. The following
poems that involve the movement from youth to old age have
been dealt with earlier in this chapter in terms of memory: "The
Bean Eaters," "On the Occasion of the Open-Air Formation of
the Olde Tymers' Walking and Nature Club," "Matthew Cole,"
and "Jessie Mitchell's Mother." In addition to these, "The Old-
marrieds," "Old Mary," and "A Sunset of the City" all include
this particular kind of negative displacement.

The couple in "The Old-marrieds" have lost either the ability
or the inclination to make love, for in spite of its being "quite a
time for loving," they did not even speak to each other. With
"Old Mary" there is a turning away from concern toward resignation. However, Old Mary does talk about "last defense," which
prompts the question, "against what?" Perhaps the same concern
for loss of glory and impending death that causes others to rely
on their memories causes her to turn to the present tense. For
the woman in "A Sunset of the City" there is an anticipation of
death. Now that her children are gone from the house and her
husband and lovers no longer find her physically attractive, she
faces the fact that she is an old woman:

> I am not deceived, I do not think it is still summer
> Because sun stays and birds continue to sing.
> . . . .

> I am a woman, and dusty, standing among new affairs.
> I am a woman who hurries through her prayers.

She looks forward to death as "dear relief" and "islanding from grief." Her dilemma is whether to die slowly or quickly: "Whether to dry/In humming pallor or to leap and die" (*World*, 337–38). This is the dilemma of all who have fallen from a glory which would cost them their lives to try to recapture.

CHAPTER 5

The Labyrinth

MISS Brooks's poetry depicts an elaborate system that has evolved in the United States which makes black people's movement in the direction of dignity and freedom overwhelmingly perilous and bewildering. This system, or labyrinth, is characterized by myriad pitfalls, dead ends, endless wrong choices, and other hazards, and the poet refers figuratively to it as the "way back home" or "Mecca", or alludes to a spiritual return to Africa which is consistently depicted as the embodiment of original dignity and freedom for the black man. It is the tortuous road that lies between spiritual death and spiritual rebirth. Though mainly concerned with expressing the psychological aspects of the labyrinth, she makes extensive use of the physical environment. The poetry abounds with images from the physical environment such as apartment buildings, halls, doors, rooms, streets, alleys, paths, stairways, and many others that represent the mad wandering in the black ghetto.

Although Gwendolyn Brooks's poetry deals largely with the various kinds of confusion experienced by the black man as a result of his fall from glory and the duplicity of the system that perpetuates his spiritual death, some attention is given to the related confusion of the white man.

The system is, after all, foisted on both blacks and whites by the tradition in the United States which evolved from a philosophy that conceives of blacks as inferior and therefore unfit for racial mixture with European-Americans.[1] So Miss Brooks's Mississippi mother is in a way as much a victim of the larger labyrinth as is the Bronzeville mother.

The philosophy behind the preconceived socially inherited notion that blacks are inferior to whites and must therefore be avoided socially as much as possible exists side by side with the philosophical platitudes of the American creed which say that all men are created equal and have certain inalienable rights.

The attempt to fulfill both diametrically opposed philosophies is the basis for the duplicity of whites and the dissembling of blacks and the confusion and self-delusion of both whites and blacks. Because, for instance, the doctrine of Manifest Destiny is quietly and efficiently being fulfilled while it is generally and overtly being denounced, because the professed white abhorrence of racial mixing peacefully coexists with the blatant testimony of extensive white-imposed miscegenation, and because the United States persists in perceiving itself as a pseudopodic extension of Europe while claiming uniqueness of national character, whites dealing with (as opposed to merely living with) blacks is a very basic, complex and confusing national problem.[2]

This problem of national schizophrenia is reflected in Miss Brooks's poetry mainly from a black perspective on the involvement with a labyrinth. As part of the blacks' continuing hell, the labyrinth often places a greater burden on them than on the whites because the whites' extreme schizoid tendencies cause the blacks' environment to shift positions constantly and to be filled with ironies and paradoxes. The system ironically forces blacks to be much more discriminating than whites. With whites discrimination is very often whimsical, while with blacks it is a matter of survival.[3] The extreme duplicity of life in race-related matters in the United States makes the task of discriminating very difficult and very often overwhelming. The heralded American experience becomes the United States experiment to blacks who, like trapped experimental rats unable to perceive a consistent pattern of successful response, spin in bewildered circles and die. To avoid the ensuing psychoses that develop with such perpetually frustrating situations, black people often look for accommodating shortcuts like categorizing all whites as enemies or always dissembling at a level that is disarming.[4] Miss Brooks not only reveals the labyrinth but records the blacks' efforts to cope with it. Hence, some poems depict characters who are merely confused and others show characters groping for the best formula to solve the labyrinth.

I *Institutional and Social Racism*

In Miss Brooks's poetry the confusion of whites is related invariably to their own prejudices. Emphasizing the unrealistic nature of white preconceptions about blacks, the poem depicts white characters experiencing some kind of rude awakening concerning their own beliefs. Sometimes the prejudice is institutional and sometimes it is social, but in every case a definite air of superiority is exhibited by the whites. An example of institutional prejudice is afforded by the attitude of the white troops before they had seen the black troops in "The White Troops Had Their Orders But the Negroes Looked Like Men." The title clearly indicates that institutional authority was involved in the preparation of the men for a situation where black troops would be present. The first three lines further illustrate the invovement of the institutional authority and the need the whites had to devise a "formula" to cope with the situation:

> They had supposed their formula was fixed
> They had obeyed instructions to devise
> A type of cold, a type of hooded gaze.

The "hooded gaze" suggests blindness and the fact that the men "had obeyed instructions" is evidence that the blindness is deliberately foisted on the white troops.[5] The poet by the presentation of these circumstances indicts the institution of the armed forces for fostering racism in its own ranks. The failure of this deliberate blindness is predictable:

> But when the Negroes came they were perplexed.
> These Negroes looked like men. Besides, it taxed
> Time and the Temper to remember those
> Congenital iniquities that cause
> Disfavor of the darkness.

Another very subtle indictment of the institutional racism is made when the poet compares the effort to prescribe the feelings of men according to race with the boxing and distribution of uniforms and other equipment. As the contents of the boxes of equipment would sometimes accidentally be "scrambled or even switched" among men of both races, so also are certain feelings scrambled among men of both races. The poem implies that anyone proceeding to prescribe feeling to people on the basis of race will encounter labyrinthian confusion. The point of the comparison is strengthened when the poet suggests that the men themselves as well as the earth, heaven, and the weather are unsympathetic toward the unnatural efforts of the institutional authority:

> Who really gave two figs?
> Neither the earth nor heaven ever trembled.
> And there was nothing startling in the weather. (*World*, 54)

There is a similar deemphasis on the indictment of the individuals as opposed to the indictment of the institution that coerces compliance to prejudice with its strictures in "A Bronzeville Mother Loiters in Mississippi. Meanwhile, a Mississippi Mother Burns Bacon." This poem relates the feelings of the white woman in Mississippi on the first day after her husband's acquittal for the murder of Emmett Till, a fourteen-year-old black youth from Chicago who supposedly made sexual advances toward the woman. Miss Brooks immediately sets the stage for the ultimate rude awakening of the heroine:

> From the first it had been like a
> Ballad. It had the beat inevitable. It had the blood.
> A wildness cut up, and tied in little bunches,
> Like the four-line stanzas of the ballads she had
>   never quite
> Understood—the ballads they had set her to,
>   in school.

"They had set her to" suggests a carefully controlled imposition of ideas rather than an active seeking of information. Again the "boxing" of human feelings according to race proves to be confusing. She conceives of herself as "the milk-white maid . . . pursued by the Dark Villain. Rescued by the Fine Prince." When the "Dark Villain" [6] turned out to be only a young boy, the unreality of her concept of the world became evident to her:

> The one thing in the world that she did know and knew
> with terrifying clarity was that her composition
> Had disintegrated. That, although the pattern
>   prevailed,
> The breaks were everywhere. That she could think
> of no thread capable of the necessary
> Sew-work.

Her rude awakening must not be construed as having eliminated her confusion. It merely confirms to her that the world she had imagined was unreal and that the confusion about it was justified. She is still faced with the task of making some order out of the shattered pieces. There is evidence that both the husband and the wife begin to doubt that the murder was worthwhile. She feels, for instance, that "it was necessary to be more beautiful than ever" so that he would "never conclude that she had not been worth it." He is nervous and fidgety and bothered by headlines in northern newspapers. He thinks about the "time lost" and "the unwanted fame." Her confusion is such that she begins to imagine that there is actually blood on her husband's hands and mouth and eventually she comes to hate him:

> She tried, but could not
> resist the idea
> That a red ooze was seeping, spreading darkly, thickly,
>   slowly
> Over her white shoulders, her own shoulders,
> And over all of Earth and Mars.
> . . . .
> But a hatred for him burst into glorious flower,
> And its perfume enclasped them—big,
> Bigger than all magnolias. (*World*, 317–24)

The poet's reference to the magnolia which calls to mind the South and its peculiarly selective "hospitality" is another subtle indictment of the influence of the institution that had enclasped them but which now leaves them full of doubts and fears about themselves and ideology of the institution.

Another instance of prejudice exhibited by individuals representing an institution is found in "The Lovers of the Poor." Both the tone and the technique in this poem help to illustrate the prejudice-induced labyrinth as they reveal the utter duplicity of the white women from the Ladies' Betterment League who very condescendingly come to the ghetto to give money to the poor. The persona's sarcastic tone is shown by the technique of placing contrasting words and phrases in close proximity to each other. The faces of ladies are described, for instance, as "seamed faces with mercy and murder hinting." The mercy refers to the overt act of giving money as perceived by the ladies themselves. The persona perceives it is another form of the continuing murder,

for these are the women of the same class that exploit the blacks
and perpetuate the very squalor they are coming to relieve. It is
highly ironic to use "the innocence of fear" to describe this bold
and predaceous class, but its veracity stems from the imagination of the white ladies who like the Mississippi mother have
fantasized a world where they are prima donnas. Further
description of the ladies includes:

> Cutting with knives served by their softest care,
> Served by their love, so barbarously fair.
> . . . .
> Herein they kiss and coddle and assault
> Anew and dearly in the innocence
> With which they baffle nature.

The poet hints strongly here that a situation so fraught with
paradoxes is bound to be confusing to everyone involved.

The ladies have come to give money to the poor, who in the
prejudiced minds of the ladies should fit the following description:

> The worthy poor. The very very worthy
> And beautiful poor. Perhaps just not too swarthy?
> Perhaps just not too dirty nor too dim
> Nor—passionate. In truth, what they could wish
> Is—something less than derelict or dull.
> Not staunch enough to stab, though, gaze for gaze!
> God shield them sharply from the beggar-bold!
> The noxious needy ones whose battle's bald
> Nonetheless for being voiceless, hits one down.

When the black poor do not conform to their preconceived notions of what the poor should be, they are horrified:

> Their League is allotting largesse to the Lost.
> But to put their clean, their pretty money, to put
> Their money collected from delicate rose-fingers
> Tipped with their hundred flawless rose-nails seems. . .
> . . . .
> Oh Squalor! This sick four-story hulk, this fibre
> With fissures everywhere! Why, what are bringings
> Of loathe-love largesse! What shall peril hungers
> So old old, what shall flatter the desolate? (*World*, 333–36)

II *The Physical World of the Labyrinth*

It is not uncommon in Miss Brooks's poetry to encounter the use of the physical surrounding as an adjunct to a theme. In this poem, as in many others, an apartment building is the setting and the poet often uses the building and its parts as images of the labyrinth. The building is equated to squalor in the above reference and is closely associated with the perplexed questions that follow it and also with the reference to. "the puzzled wreckage of the middle passage." Halls particularly are referred to in this poem as things navigated precariously at best. Shortly after entering the apartment building, the ladies are said to "walk in a gingerly manner up the hall." Near the end of the poem the retreat of the ladies from the building is described thus:

> Keeping their scented bodies in the center
> Of the hall as they walk down the hysterical hall,
> They allow their lovely skirts to graze no wall.

Here, as in many of Miss Brooks's poems, halls are definite images of the labyrinth—suggesting chaos and danger. More instances of halls and other entities used as images of the labyrinth will be presented later in this chapter.[7]

The poet also often uses streets, alleys, paths, and other traversable entities as images of the labyrinth along with images of light and dark, sight and blindness relating to the ease or difficulty of negotiation. The opening lines of "The Lovers of the Poor" afford a good example of labyrinthian imagery:

> The Lovers of the Poor
>   arrive. The Ladies from the Ladies' Betterment
> League
> Arrive in the afternoon, the late light slanting
> In diluted gold bars across the boulevard.

The ladies have arrived late—after squalor and misery is rampant —after noon, the brightest time of the day. The late light is "slanting" and "diluted," suggesting its indirectness and weakness. These gold bars, this "largesse to the Lost," is what they bring slanting across the boulevard which needs a much stronger and more earnest light. With these lines the poet has aptly introduced the ironic fiasco that follows. The ladies flee, taking with them their "loathe-love," which is Miss Brooks's term for the investment they were to make ostensibly in the betterment of the poor. After repeating the sanctimonious title, she uses the term "better" with ironic effect to the ladies' own rationale for fleeing:

> The Ladies from the Ladies'
> Betterment League agree it will be better
> To achieve the outer air that rights and steadies,
> To hie to a house that does not holler, to ring
> Bells elsetime, better presently to cater
> To no more Possibilities, to get
> Away. (*World*, 333, 336)

Because the real investment was to be in themselves for the assuagement of their guilt, the poet convincingly implies that they are lovers only of themselves and "loathers of the poor."

An example of a more personal level of prejudice and its resultant confusion is provided by "Bronzeville Woman in a Red Hat." Here a black woman is hired as a last resort to be a maid in the household of a Mrs. Miles. Mrs. Miles's prejudice is immediately obvious as she reflects on the black maid's presence in the house:

> They had never had one in the house before.
>   The strangeness of it all. Like unleashing
> A lion, really, Poised
> To pounce. A puma. A panther, A black
> Bear.
> There it stood in the door,
> Under a red hat that was rash, but refreshing—
> In a tasteless way, of course—across the dull dare,
> The semi-assault of that extraordinary blackness.
> . . . .
> There it stood
> In the door. They had never had
> One in the house before.

Reference to the black woman as "it" and as several kinds of wild animals is a clear indication of Mrs. Miles's negative attitude. When her child is kissed by the maid, her preconceived idea of the natural arrangement of the world is shaken:

World yelled, world writhed, world turned to light
            and rolled
Into her kitchen, nearly knocked her down.

She thinks momentarily that her child is confused and lost in a labyrinthian situation:

She, quite supposing purity despoiled,
Committed to sourness, disordered, soiled,
Went in to pry the ordure form the cream
Cooing, "Come." (Come out of the cannibal wilderness,
Dirt, dark, into the sun and bloomful air.
Return to freshness of your right world, wear
Sweetness again. Be done with beast, duress.)

A greater, almost unbearable, shock was in store for her when her child clung to and kissed back the black maid. At this point she begins to suspect that she is herself out of tune with the natural order of things:

Heat at the hairline, heat between the bowels,
Examining seeming coarse unnatural scene,
She saw all things except herself serene:
Child, big black woman, pretty kitchen towels. (*World*, 351–54)

There is in "I Love Those Little Booths at Benvenuti's" a definite sense by whites of being betrayed by blacks who do not perform in accordance with the prejudices of the whites. As in "The Lovers of the Poor," whites voluntarily visit the black ghetto. In this poem they are doing what is commonly called "slumming;" that is, visiting the black ghetto to observe blacks exhibit all the traits that they are "supposed" to have.

The whites in this poem want to sit in the booths at Benvenuti's inconspicuously and watch blacks be "clamorous," "colorfully incorrect," "amorous," "flatly brave," "dirty," "carmine," "hot," sexually uninhibited, prayerful, "partial," and "unpretty." When the black people do none of the things which the whites had been sure blacks always do, the whites react in this way:

They stare, They tire, They feel refused,
Feel overwhelmed by subtle treason!
Nobody here will take the part of jester.

> The absolute stutters, and the rationale
> Stoops off in astonishment.
> But not gaily
> And not with their consent. (*World*, 111)

Miss Brooks presents here yet another example of whites being led into the labyrinth by their own prejudices. The rude awakening or reversal in each case is tantamount to shaking if not shattering the neatly stereotypical fantasy worlds of the white characters.

There are blacks also who are in a state of general confusion which often is directly related to the prejudice-based confusion of whites. Some of Miss Brooks's poetry depicts blacks in situations in which they do not necessarily seek answers to the labyrinth but rather merely reflect on their thunderstruck condition or express awe in the face of chaos.

"The Last Quatrain of the Ballad of Emmett Till" is really a sequel to "A Bronzeville Mother Loiters in Mississippi. Meanwhile, a Mississippi Mother Burns Bacon." Emmett's mother, the Bronzeville mother of the other poem, sits numbly and remembers her killed boy:

> Emmett's mother is a pretty-faced thing;
>   the tint of pulled taffy.
> She sits in a red room
>   drinking black coffee.
> She kisses her killed boy.
>   and she is sorry.
> Chaos in windy grays
>   through a red prairie. (*World*, 324)

The poet, meanwhile, plays with colors as if merely fingering the key that will open a lock; however, the taffy, red, black, gray, and red again lead nowhere, emphasizing the chaos. The chaos in turn magnifies the numbness of the mother, who the poet says, in masterful understatement, sits, drinks, remembers, and is sorry. Some part of her mind is aware of the surrounding red carnage and that she is as powerless as death to fathom it or change it.

A similar kind of helpless impotence is expressed by Lester in "Strong Men Riding Horses." Here the poet's comments on a black man's reaction to the heroic image of white men as "Strong

Men" evinces the centrality of the ghetto dweller's inability to identify with his environment. They (white men) are seen by Lester as strong, brave, and too saddled to flinch from a challenge. His self-deprecation is expressed in these lines: "I am not like that. I pay rent, am addled/By illegible landlords, run, if robbers call" (*World*, 313). The apartment building–rent syndrome again is evident as a reference to the spiritual death, for he is "addled" as opposed to being "saddled" and expresses awe toward the "rentless" white men.[8]

Beyond all the capricious befuddlements of the rich white women of the Ladies' Betterment League in "The Lovers of the Poor," Miss Brooks, in her description of the victims of the squalor, alludes to the overall labyrinth confronted by the black man: ". . . The puzzled wreckage of the middle passage, and urine and stale shames" (*World*, 336). This passage is an allusion to the squalid misery of the slaves on the ships sailing between West Africa and America during the American slave-trade period which suggests that these black victims are inheritors of the "puzzled wreckage" even as the rich ladies are inheritors of the power to exploit and enslave in the name of betterment.

That the labyrinthian condition is part of the black man's inheritance is expressed also in "Old Laughter," which is a general statement of the history of the black man passing from glory to ruin. The phrase "in bright, bewildered Africa" refers to the continuing condition of confusion of African people everywhere.

"Men of Careful Turns, Haters of Forks in the Road" draws into perspective the general goal of the black man and depicts from the black man's point of view some of the psychological wile used by the white man in at once thwarting and placating the black man. The result constitutes a slice of the labyrinthian experience. "Forks in the road" necessitate choices and are therefore hated by the people in the labyrinth.[9] "The strain at the eye, that puzzlement, that awe" indicates the fear each arouses because it allows a chance for a wrong turn. As part of the experience of the labyrinth the black man's supplication includes a request to be treated as an equal and makes a comparison of the relationship of white and black men to that of lovers. In the analogy the drunken carelessness of the white mate suggests a confusing whimsicality. The black man points out part of the wile of the system which replaces crude bigotry with discreet bigotry and names the change progress. He says the white man tries to calm him by telling him that prejudice is natural and that "politeness will take care of what needs caring." He is also told that he must recognize the "long and electric" line that meaningfully separates black and white and that he must never transgress it. The black man obviously recognizes the schemes of the white man to constrain him, but his admonishing rejoinder is to realize that the both of them are lost and must combine to find by their own wits a way to true brotherhood. The poet's own words portentously allude to the labyrinth: "We are lost, must/ Wizard a track through our own screaming weed" (*World*, 124). The conclusion is that since they both are lost, the only solution is through a cooperative effort. However, because the navigation must be accomplished without the help of "magics or elves or timely godmothers" and because they must "wizard" through "screaming weed" the anticipated difficulty seems probable.

To some of Miss Brooks's characters the toll of the "puzzled wreckage of the middle passage," the unsolvable labyrinth, is so overwhelming that they consider the possibility of suicide.[10] The woman who is aware of growing older and less needed by her family and lovers in "A Sunset of the City" considers suicide as a possible solution of her problem. She maintains that she is not deceived; she is aware of the "indrying and dying down" and of the closeness of winter of death. But she does confess a confusion about what she can do to alleviate her grief at being an anachronism to life:

> I am cold in this cold house this house
> Whose washed echoes are tremulous down lost halls.
> I am a woman, and dusty, standing among new affairs.
> I am a woman who hurries through her prayers.

"Down lost halls" is used as an image of the labyrinth as she tries to find an answer to her "dual dilemma":

> Whether to dry
> In humming pallor or to leap and die. (*World*, 338)

"A man of the Middle Class" similarly feels "dusty: and out of place and confused among new affairs." Speaking of his situation he says:

> I am bedraggled, with sundry dusts to be shed;
> Trailing desperate tarnished tassels. These
>   strident Aprils
> With terrifying polkas and Bugle Calls
> Confound me. (*World*, 339)

He reflects on his success in acquiring material wealth and possessions and remarks how he had loved directions and orders. Bemoaning his impotence, he indicates that he has everything but answers. The only answer he has is to do what other executives have done—shoot himself or jump to his death—but he has not yet come to the point of doing it himself.

It seems to be the search for answers in coping with feelings of impotence and worthlessness that induces people in some of Miss Brooks's poems to consider suicide as a possible solution. "The Contemplation of Suicide: The Temptation of Timothy" shows a person asking questions about the meaning of life:

> One poises, poses, at tract, or range, or river,
> Saying, What is the fact of my life, to what do I
>   tend?—
> And is it assured and sweet that I have come, after
>   mazes
> And robins, after the foodless swallowings and
>   snatchings
> At fog, to this foppish end? (*World*, 355)

The implication is that although life has involved the labyrinth, pleasure, and frustration, it is worthy of more than a selfish suicide. The persona in this poem decides that he wants to continue to be part of many-faceted life.

III   *Surviving in the Labyrinth*

The poet includes other poems dealing with general confusion induced by the labyrinth in which characters make efforts or express desires to survive in the labyrinth while protesting it or trying to navigate it. "People Protest in Sprawling Lightless Ways" illustrates this precarious balance between protest and survival. People are said to "abort their furies" and "save their censures and their damns" against their deceivers. "Sprawling" and "Lightless" imply that the protests are "without form" or intelligence. Man makes a frantic plea to anyone to be his reviver. The complexity and confusion of the labyrinth cause him to "follow many a cloven foot." The image of "cloven foot" suggests the many devils that pursue and are pursued as the black man tries to escape the labyrinth of his hell.

Among those people who arm themselves for the fights of this world, there are those who search for an absolute truth for formula that would be workable in all situations. The poet includes this fight and this search in a number of poems. In "Garbageman: The Man with Orderly Mind" the poet makes use of the image of the garbageman whose planned route is evidence of "sterling" sense of direction. This man, who regularly plies the course of the labyrinthian chartered streets in orderly fashion, is revered and consulted like an oracle by the persona who represents those trapped helpless in the labyrinth:

> What do you think of us in fuzzy endeavor, you whose
>   directions are sterling, whose lunge is straight?
> Can you make a reason, how can you pardon us who
>   memorize the rules and never score?
> Who memorize the rules from your own text but never
>   quite transfer them to the game,
> Who never quite receive the whistling ball, who gawk,
>   begin to absorb the crowd's own roar. (*SP*, 124)

Light here is used as an image of wisdom and right direction, as it is in many of Miss Brooks's poems. Neither light nor earnestness alone is enough to solve the labyrinth, nor are both together adequate for those who merely cry out in bewilderment against the dark. What is also needed is aggressive, straight-lunging endeavor, or fighting, as depicted in the next two poems.

The poet makes a similar statement in "Weaponed Woman" about the relation of light to combating the confusion of the labyrinth:

> Well, life has been a baffled vehicle
> And baffling. But she fights, and
> Has fought, according to her lights and
> The lenience of her whirling-place. (*SP*, 125)

"According to her lights" should be interpreted as "in the best way she knew how." The lenience suggests the necessary awareness of the ultimate control of the situation by the "foster designers," white men, who control all her climates. "Whirling-place" is used ambiguously as a place in which to whirl and as a place which is whirling. Her weapons are semifolded arms which imply a stubborn patience, her strongbag which is the trademark of work-ladies, and the stiff frost of her face which indicates her strong will and determination "that challenges 'When' and 'If.'"

"Big Bessie Throws Her Son into the Street" pictures another woman who has fought well and is now forcing her son to face the labyrinth using his own wiles. She admonishes her son to fight the labyrinth with wisdom and will:

> Be precise.
> With something better than candles in the eyes.
> (Candles are not enough.)
> At the root of the will, a wild inflammable stuff.

The "wild inflammable stuff" "at the root of the will" is the same as the "stiff frost" in the face of the weaponed woman and the "earnestness" of the garbageman. Her final admonition to him is:

> New pioneer of days and ways, be gone.
> Hunt out your own or make your own alone.
>
> Go down the street. (*SP*, 127)

She admonishes him to search out his own way, hopefully more precisely (like the straight-lunging garbageman) than she had been able to search with only candles in her eyes. It is appropriate that she "throws" her son, for the term connotes her confidence that he is as ready as she can make him to survive in the labyrinth which is suggested here by "the street" as it is in other poems. In "Do Not Be Afraid of No," for instance, where a young girl is admonished not to choose the path of prostitution simply because of the cheap material comforts it can bring, street and light imagery are used to illustrate the pitfalls of the labyrinthian occupation:

> Stupid, like a street
> That beats into a dead end and dies there, with
> nothing left to reprimand or meet.

> And like a candle fixed
> Against dismay and countershine of mixed
>
> Wild moon and sun. And like
> A flying furniture, or bird with lattice wing; or
>> gaunt thing,
>> a-stammer down a nightmare neon peopled with
>> condor, hawk and shrike. (*World*, 76)

The "dead end" implies a trap that precludes correct choices and the candle implies too puny a light, pitted against "wild moon and sun," for successfully plying the labyrinth. Her predicted clumsy ineptness on the street is also portentous of her failure.

The positive admonition expressed in "Garbageman: The Man with the Orderly Mind," "Weaponed Woman," and "Big Bessie Throws Her Son into the Street" involves precision of endeavor, light or wisdom and strong will or earnestness. This kind of admonition takes a turn toward verbal chastisement in "Leftist Orator in Washington Park Pleasantly Punishes the Gropers." The orator first acknowledges that he understands their amazement at the "crazy snow" that represents the unreadable, addling white designers of the climate. He warns that conditions will not get better: "I am afraid the wind will not falter at any time in the night." He also understands that the blacks are frightened and bewildered. He foretells that conditions will get much worse, approaching desperation: "I foretell the heat and yawn of eye and the drop of the mouth and the screech,/The foolish, unhappy screech hanging high on the air." He blames this future calamity on black lack of "dream or belief or reach." Whereas "Garbageman: The Man with the Orderly Mind" ask questions, "Is light enough (to solve the labyrinth) when this bewilderment crying against the dark shuts down the shades?" The orator asserts that the reason for the worsening befuddllement and ruin will be "because you would only screech." Again the poet implies that light or wisdom, precise endeavor in the "sterling" direction, and earnestness or strong will are needed to prevent the otherwise likely worsening of black conditions:

> Because you were nothing, saw nothing, did
>> nothing at all.
> Because there will be No Thing for which
>> you fall. (*World*, 364)

Providing a departure from the admonitions and the verbal chastisements, Miss Brooks's poetry also presents the labyrinth from the perspectives of those suffering from its debilitating torments. The effect of the weight of having ceaselessly to search through the labyrinth is expressed in the opening lines of "One Wants a Teller in a Time Like This:"

> One's not a man, one's not a woman grown,
> To bear enormous business all alone.
>
> One cannot walk this winding street with pride,
> Straight-shouldered, tranquil-eyed,
> Knowing one knows for sure the way back home.
> One wonders if one has a home.

Conveyed here is the idea that the responsibility should be shared by the black people as a whole, that it is too much to bear without the support of others. The "winding street" is an image of the labyrinth which precludes actual black pride, black virility, black peace of mind, or black certainty about anything. This uncertainty is further implied in the next lines: "One is not certain if or why or how/One wants a Teller now:—" The prescription for remedy of the "beautiful disease" is to apply the blindfold of faith by reaching out for and subscribing to the nearest absolute available. This prescription reinforces the prop used at the beginning of the poem which illustrates the shame one feels at not being able to fulfill his or her concept of manhood or womanhood. The ravages of the "winding street" tempt one to abort his movement toward maturity and assume the role (and therefore the lesser responsibility) of a child. Hence the prescription is given as if to a child:

> *Put on your rubbers and you won't catch cold.*
> *Here's hell, there's heaven. Go to Sunday School.*
> *Be patient, time brings all good things*—(and cool
> Strong balm to calm the burning at the brain?)—
> *Behold,*
> *Love's true, and triumphs; and God's actual.* (World, 116)

Each of the suggestions, besides being appropriate for a child, is simple, unequivocal, and rather reliable once certain basic premises are accepted a priori. The unitalicized "cool strong balm to calm the burning at the brain" cleaves through clearly as the handy adult gloss to explain the italicized script used for the necessary child-therapy play. The poet expresses not only the relentless frustration involved in trying to run the maze but also the extreme elusiveness of effective therapy for black adults in a society that strongly resists black maturity by innumerable conscious and subconscious stratagems.

The effort to run the maze is interrupted only by the quest for rest which becomes part of the labyrinth itself. In "The Explorer" as in "One Wants a Teller in a Time Like This," relief is sought from the constant responsibility of finding the way back home. The explorer's very wish "to find a still spot in the noise," however, is itself described as frayed:

> So tipping down the scrambled halls he set
> vague hands on throbbing knobs. There were behind
> Only spiraling, high human voices,
> The scream of nervous affairs,
> Wee griefs,
> Grand griefs. And choices.
>
> He feared most of all the choices, that cried to be
>   taken.
> There were no bourns.
> There were no quiet rooms. (*World*, 311)

He fears most the choices crying to be taken because they are invitations to continue the search for the solution of the labyrinth, the endeavor from which he is trying to find relief. The labyrinth is suggested in this poem by a number of images including "noise," "din," "Frayed hope," "Winding," "hunting," "room," "scrambled halls," "vague hands on throbbing knobs," "spiraling," "the scream of nervous affairs," and "choices." Most of these images would connote confusion or the labyrinth independently but others borrow meaning from the context.

Perhaps the persona provides hypothetical relief at least in "Truth" by supposing that the mystery of the labyrinth were suddenly solved. She ostensibly speculates that people would dread "sun" after being in the shade so long. She states that in spite of having cried for wisdom and right direction, it still might be that people would really prefer "the dear thick shelter of the familiar propitious haze." She ends the poem with a statement about the security of the shade or labyrinth:

> Sweet is it, sweet is it
> To sleep in the coolness
> Of snug unawareness.
>
> The dark hangs heavily
> Over the eyes. (*World*, 114)

The poem may be suggesting the possibility that awareness may be attended by greater responsibilities than "snug unawareness."

A more likely approach to this poem, however, is to see it as a more subtle companion to the admonition found in "Garbageman: The Man with the Orderly Mind," "Big Bessie Throws Her Son into the Street," and "Leftist Orator in Washington Park Pleasantly Punishes the Gropers." The suggestion to black people that they may be happier confused than they are facing the truth about their continuing subjugation is an insult. But insults goad. An insult just might be the spark to ignite the "wild inflammable stuff" "at the root of the will" that Big Bessie speaks about. It might excite the earnestness mentioned in "Garbageman: The Man with the Orderly Mind" and inspire a cause for which a people might fall (or rise) as referred to by the leftist orator.

Others who grope for a way out of the labyrinth seek ones that will be successful not only for them but for others like them. A big frustration is trying to find a path traversable by a person and his loved ones. Miss Brooks's poetry deals with the protection and arming of children, for instance, not just against death or evil in general, but against the uncertainties of the frightening riddles of the labyrinth in particular.[11] Most of these poems appear in one consecutive series of sonnets entitled "The Children of the Poor." The first of these poems, "People Who Have No Children Can Be Hard," sets the special concerns of parents apart from those of others. The opening octave complains that people who have no children can live recklessly and die without the extra burden of providing protection for them and can afford to defy the labyrinth or to "leap and die" if they choose. The sestet illustrates that with parents, however, the helplessness of the children makes a trap which is also a curse. The labyrinth comes into play when poor parents begin searching for weapons and devices to give their children so that they can navigate life with the least amount of damage. The second poem of this group directly addresses itself to this question. "What Shall I Give My Children? Who Are Poor" depicts in its octave a parent who feels helpless to give his child "a brisk contour" and a feeling that black is not inferior:

> What shall I give my children: who are poor,
> Who are adjudged the leastwise of the land,
> . . . .
> But who have begged me for a brisk contour,
> Crying that they are quasi, contraband
> Because unfinished, graven by a hand
> Less than angelic, admirable or sure.

The sestet shows the parent using what wiles he can to provide answers, blindfolds, and general protection for the children's self-esteem but finding that the world (the climate) speaks so much louder and more convincingly that the children of the poor come to concur with those who adjudge them "least-wise of the land:" [12]

> My hand is stuffed with mode, design, device.
> But I lack access to my proper stone,
> And plenitude of plan shall not suffice
> Nor grief nor love shall be enough alone
> To ratify my little halves who bear
> Across an autumn freezing everywhere. (*World*, 100)

Something more is needed to supplement the assurances of the parent, that the children are not "graven by a hand less than angelic, admirable or sure."

A third poem, "And Shall I Prime My Children, Pray, to Pray?" illustrates another attempt to solve the problem of girding children of the poor for the pitfalls and dead ends of life's labyrinth. Specifically, the parent is questioning the efficacy of religion and whether or not the rigors and inhibitions are worthwhile. The parent's negative terms for referring to religion suggest that he himself is not a believer but is willing to try religion as an answer for his children. For example, "all hysterics arrogant for a day," "confine your lights in jellied rules," "resemble graves," and "be metaphysical mules" are all suggestive of the stultifying conditions of religion. The sestet indicates the neatness of the motif appeal, however, because it should preclude the need for disturbing questions. Nevertheless, the parent will stand by ready to intercede at any time:

> Behind the scurryings of your neat motif
> I shall wait, if you wish: revise the psalm
> If that should frighten you: sew up belief
> If that should tear: turn, singularly calm
> At forehead and at fingers rather wise,
> Holding the bandage ready for your eyes. (*World*, 101)

The perplexing nature of the labyrinth leads some to conclude that preoccupation with it is an extravagant waste of time and energy which blacks have in very limited supply. This is the answer offered in "First Fight. Then Fiddle." Fiddling is equated here to the frivolous effort of trying to ply the labyrinth:

> First fight. Then fiddle, Ply the slipping string
> With feathery sorcery; muzzle the note
> With hurting love; the music that they wrote
> Bewitch, bewilder. Qualify to sing
> Threadwise. Devise no salt, no hempen thing
> For the dear instrument to bear. Devote
> The bow to silks and honey. Be remote
> A While from malice and from murdering.

The admonition is to become proficient someday in artful dalliance abstaining from enslaving, hating, murdering. Before this luxury can be afforded, hate must be enjoyed as a chief weapon to enforce the right to be frivolous and "civilized":

> But first to arms, to armor. Carry hate
> In front of you and harmony behind.
> Be deaf to music and to beauty blind
> Win War. Rise bloody, maybe not too late
> For having first to civilize a space
> Wherein to play your violin with grace. (*World*, 102)

The final sonnet of this series is perhaps a logical sequel to "First Fight. Then Fiddle," for contemplation of death seems appropriate after an exhortation to fight a mightier enemy. "When My Dears Die" appears to try to reach beyond preparation for plying the labyrinth of life and contemplates the possibility of an order that may include death also. The question is raised as to whether there can be any consolation in the death of children when the liveliness and color are chilled "into tightness and into a remarkable politeness":

> May not they in the crisp encounter see
> Something to recognize and read as rightness?

Here there is an implication that in life the low self-esteem of those "who have begged . . . for brisk contour" and consider themselves "unfinished" may in death be corrected. In the sestet the parent is consoled by the speculation that the trials of the labyrinth itself may have conditioned the children to accept death easily:

> I say they may, so granitely discreet,
> The little crooked questionings inbound,
> Concede themselves on most familiar ground,
> Cold an old predicament of the breath;
> Adroit, the shapely prefaces complete,
> Accept the university of death. (*World*, 103)

The "little crooked questionings" connote the labyrinth while "inbound" refers to the forced acceptance of the many unaskables and unanswerables of life. Death may answer many questions that the parent could not and thereby may indeed be a "university" acceptable to the children.

The idea of "the little crooked questionings" applied outside the present world is extended in "Hunchback Girl: She Thinks of Heaven." Here as in "When My Dears Die" there is an implication that because the quest for the feeling of "rightness" cannot be fulfilled in this world, contemplation of death becomes a consolation. The words of the girl show the importance not only of feeling "right" but also of freedom from affectation and inhibition:

> My Father, it is surely a blue place
> And straight. Right. Regular. Where I shall find

No need for scholarly nonchalance or looks
A little to the left or guard upon the
Heart to halt love that runs without crookedness
Along its crooked corridors. My father,
It is a planned place surely. Out of coils,
Unscrewed, released, no more to be marvelous
I shall walk straightly through most proper halls
Proper myself, princess of properness. (*World*, 11)

Key imagery of heaven is directly opposite to that of the labyrinth. Whereas the labyrinth, for instance, is dark, crooked, conducive to wrong choices, irregular, she visualizes a "blue" "straight," "right," "regular" place. The "crooked corridors" is an image of the labyrinth, referring here to the heart curbed and channeled to conform to the labyrinth. The security of being able to address a "Father" with such familiarity and certainty implied by "surely" and "planned" negate the awesome impersonality, capriciousness, and uncertainty of the labyrinth. The girl will be uncoiled, unscrewed, free from the burden of excelling to prove one's right to be—all opposite the conditions of the labyrinth. She dreams of "walking straightly through most proper halls" as no one does in the labyrinth. How fitting that she who in life is among those "adjudged the leastwise of the land" shall in heaven be "princess of properness."

The idea of heaven's being a consolation is not appealing to everyone who suffers the devastation of the labyrinth. As if to counter the hunchback girl's expression of hope and faith, "The Certainty We Two Shall Meet by God" rejects postponement of life—even if it means that some day the two will be free of the labyrinth:

The Certainty we two shall meet by God.
In a wide Parlor, underneath a Light
Of lights, come Sometime, is no ointment now.

The terms that have direct reference to the labyrinth are capitalized for special emphasis. Although "Certainty," "Parlor," "Light of lights," and "Sometime" refer to heaven, they are attributes directly opposite from those of the labyrinth and are used similarly to the negating terms in "Hunchback Girl: She Thinks of Heaven." "Sometime" is pitted against "never" of the labyrinth. These two young people evidently feel that "now" is the only

time to negate "never." "Sometime" is inadequate because they
are "worshipers of life," wanting to enjoy all its pleasures now:

> We want nights
> Of vague adventure, lips lax wet and warm,
> Bees in the stomach, sweat across the brow. Now. (*World*, 95)

The slight suggestion of cynicism is reinforced by the statement:
"We never did learn how to find white in the Bible." With this
declaration it is evident that the couple is questioning traditional
"truths." Whether the couple is questioning the veracity of the
Bible or asserting that the white man does not seem to follow the
Bible or that his interpretation of the Bible is distinctly to his
own advantage, is perhaps purposely ambiguous, but all of these
ideas are suggested.

IV   *Masks of the Black Psyche*

At times the artful ambiguity of the poet bespeaks the complexity of the black psyche in masking to itself and the world its
real fears and concerns. Sometimes the multiplicity of overlapping and intertwined meanings reflects the complex ways in
which blacks have had to use objects of their "foster" environment to conjure out a reality from the unreality, coax pleasure
from misery. Like sailors learning to position their sails so that
they could navigate correctly against the wind, black accommo-
dation and adjustment to their social environment have often
necessitated their seeing the desert as a garden. Hence the black
ghetto is ambivalently referred to as concentration camp and as
haven for freedom. Each experience ambiguously becomes a
means of denying or forgetting the existence of oppression or of
exposing it to the extent of explaining life in terms of it. Miss
Brooks's poetry shows many parallels between the black man's
subjugation and religion, war, love, and other seemingly aracial,
social, personal, and political occurrences.
The cynicism is slightly stronger in "A Lovely Love" than it is
in "The Certainty We Two Shall Meet by God." Here traditional
values begin to come within the scope of the questioning.
Traditional moral values are indirectly being questioned by vir-
tue of the defiant defense of activities that are normally considered desecrations of these values. In fact, where the prevailing

direction of most poems on the labyrinth has been toward relief from the labyrinth, in this poem the images that connote the labyrinth are hallowed by love, indicating a reversal of traditional values.

> Let it be alleys, Let it be a hall
> Whose janitor javelins epithet and thought
> To cheapen hyacinth darkness that we sought
> And played we found, rot, make the petals fall.
>
> Let it be stairways, and a splintery box
> Where you have thrown me, scraped me with your kiss,
> Have honed me, have released me after this
> Cavern kindness, smiled away our shocks.

The fact that the love is carnal as opposed to platonic heightens the sense of reversal. Alleys, a hall, stairways, and a box in the "hyacinth darkness" are decidedly positive as used here but are intertwined with images that can be ambivalently interpreted only with great difficulty. What is positive about a janitor hurling curses at them as they make love in the hall? or about rot? or about fallen petals? It would seem only a masochist could get pleasure from a splintery box. But that box represents the ghetto, and pleasure will be had, even from the most unpleasant of sources, if more favorable choices are precluded. Black masochism is a social reality and the poet deals with it also in poems that depict contemplations of suicide and other forms of self-punishment.[13]

The sestet helps to clarify the ambiguity and the ambivalence of the preceding lines:

> That is the birthright of our lovely love
> In swaddling clothes. Not like that Other one.
> Not lit by any fondling star above.
> Not found by any wise men, either. Run.
> People are coming. They must not catch us here
> Definitionless in this strict atmosphere. (*World*, 347)

Through the obvious allusion to Christ by "in swaddling clothes," it becomes evident that the poem has religious overtones and that the most unyieldingly negative objects before are transformed into the most sacred. The splintery box and all the other negative aspects of the ghetto become the cross the black man may carry. A defiant rejection of Christ by the lovers in the poem is effected by the contemptuous reference to him as "that Other one" rather than by name. Deliberately the comparison is made in terms ironically unfavorable to Christ. The light of the "fondling star" and the wise men are relegated to a negative position by the context of the poem although they would normally have positive connotations. This reversal from positive to negative connotations balances the negative-to-positive reversal of connotations of ghetto-associated objects mentioned in the octave. The lovers are "persecuted" by the janitor who "javelins epithet and thought" and by the people from whom they run. They choose to scorn the rigid strictures of the labyrinth by enjoying their "birthright" rather than fighting it; they brazenly seek to exploit chaos, becoming "definitionless," rather than trying to solve it.

Although the use of the versatile sonnet form as an instrument of social protest has many precedents, such practice still marks something of a departure from the usual subjects associated with sonnets. The interesting variation here is that Miss Brooks does use a traditional subject and effects striking social protest by changing the values attached to the subject matter.[14] The reversals in this last sonnet of the series and the departure from the usual functions of sonnets reflect the propensity of a growing portion of the black community to reverse categorically the values of the white "foster designers" of their environment.[15] Hence white, religion, law, justice, patriotism, platonic love, and other traditionally positive entities and concepts become negative, and black, free love, revolution, retribution, and other generally negative entities and concepts assume positive attributes. In a series of other sonnets and in other poems, ostensibly dealing with religion, love, and/or war, Miss Brooks reflects the cynicism of the black man toward United States institutions and pursuits, by expressing with deft ambiguity his disillusionment, doubt, and disgust.

The cynical tone borders on sarcasm in "Firstly Inclined To Take What It Is Told." The tone suggests bitterness and disenchantment:

> Thee sacrosanct, Thee sweet, Thee crystalline,
> With the full jewel wile of mighty light—

> With the narcotic milk of peace for men
> Who find Thy beautiful center and relate
> Thy round command, Thy grand, Thy mystic good—
> Thee like the classic quality of a star:
> A little way from warmth, a little sad,
> Delicately lovely to adore. . . .

The profusion of "thees" and "thys" constitutes a mockery of biblical idiom and a more subtle derision through false and exaggerated expression of reverence for God. Contrasting terms in close proximity hint that the meaning is not altogether straight-forward. "Wile of mighty light" combines a negative image of labyrinthian trickery (wile) with a positive image of labyrinthian relief (mighty light). The same clash occurs with "narcotic milk of peace." "Narcotic milk" itself contains incongruous terms to the extent that "narcotic" is a camouflage for pain as well as a relaxer and milk is one of the most basic sustainers of life.[16] "Peace" and the "mighty light" are the apparent rewards that relieve the agonies of the labyrinth: "narcotic" and "wile" hint at the poisonous treachery of religion and "milk" and "jewel" are the enticements—the baits attached in imagery to a pervasive need or want of men. This kind of attachment recalls "jellied rules" in "And Shall I Prime My Children, Pray, to Pray?" "Mystic good" is in contrast to practical, earthly good. The comparison to a classic star further suggests its remoteness in time and distance and "delicately" suggests its fragility that would be vulnerable to the handling of rough and desperate men. The subtle implica-tion is that religion's excessive impracticality makes it not only worthless for the black man in the labyrinth but indeed, with its narcotic wiles, part of the labyrinth itself.

As usual in her sonnets, Miss Brooks uses the sestet to explain or resolve the problem presented in the octave:

> I had been brightly ready to believe.
> For youth is a frail thing, not unafraid.
> Firstly inclined to take what it is told,
> Firstly inclined to lean. Greedy to give
> Faith tidy and total. To a total God.
> With billowing heartiness no whit withheld. (*World*, 55)

The past-perfect tense of the verb "had been" indicates that the state of readiness to believe is over. Inexperience and fear had prompted the readiness to believe, to be fully dependent. "Tidy and total" echoes the "neat motif" referred to in "And Shall I Prime My Children, Pray, to Pray?" The ending confirms the overall tone of bitter disillusionment.

The second sonnet of the series, " 'God Works in a Mysterious Way,' " continues the statement of disillusionment with religion. In this poem the impressionable, fearful youth of "Firstly Inclined To Take What It Is Told" has given way to a skeptical, willful, and bolder youth, as the octave clearly shows:

> But often now the youthful eye cuts down its
> Own dainty veiling. Or submits to winds.
> And many an eye that all its age had drawn its
> Beam from a Book endures the impudence
> Of modern glare that never heard of tact
> Or timeliness, or Mystery that shrouds
> Immortal joy: It merely can direct
> Chancing feet across dissembling clods.

The suspension of disbelief is not so readily achieved as in times past and the Bible comes under open attack. Tact, timeliness, or blind, obedient reverence for the "Mystery that shrouds immortal joy" are also too "dainty" to protect religion from the "impudence of modern glare." The light and sight imagery, which suggests the labyrinth, shows a progression away from blindness toward sight. "The youthful eye" first "cuts down its own dainty veiling" or removes its blindness. Next the eyes of those whose "beam" (of light) had come from the Bible is exposed to the glare (of light or insight) from the youthful eye. Significantly the past-perfect tense of the verb "had drawn" indicates that they no longer draw their beams from the Bible. "The modern glare" can direct the lost (chancing feet) through the labyrinth (dissembling clods). The exhortation in the sestet is for God to reveal himself in deeds of retribution and correction:

> Out from Thy shadows, from Thy pleasant meadows,
> Quickly, in undiluted light. Be glad, whose
> Mansions are bright, to right thy children's air.
> If Thou be more than hate or atmosphere
> Step forth in splendor, mortify our wolves,
> Or we assume a sovereignty ourselves. (*World*, 56)

The "shadows" and "pleasant meadows" as place of hiding are images of the labyrinth as is the "undiluted light." Miss Brooks uses darkness and shadows to represent the condition of the labyrinth, diluted light is associated with a puny or false effort to solve the labyrinth, and glare or undiluted light or the equivalent represents the wisdom necessary to ply the labyrinth. "Right thy children's air" and "mortify our wolves" is a demand in the name of justice to correct the social evils perpetrated on blacks. The last line, "Or we assume a sovereignty ourselves," forewarns of the reversals as depicted in "A Lovely Love."

The next sonnet, "Love Note I: Surely," is a masterful example of a meaningful mesh of content and technique. This is a poem about doubt, and the multiplicity of possible referents lends itself to a display of artful ambiguity. Examination of the octave reveals that the identity of the addressee in this poem is not clear:

> Surely you stay my certain own, you stay
> My you. All honest, lofty as a cloud
> Surely I could come now and find you high,
> As mine as you ever were; should not be awed.
> Surely your word would pop as insolent
> As always: "Why, of course I love you, dear."
> Your gaze, surely, ungauzed as I could want.
> Your touches, that never were careful, what they were.

Is the persona addressing a lover or the country represented by a flag? The very personal tone conveyed by "you" suggests that the addressee is a lover. "My certain own" also suggests a personal relationship. "Lofty as a cloud" and "high" hint that a flag might be the object of attention. The insolent assurance of love seems appropriate for a lover; however, it is possible that the lover motif is used to suggest the relationship between a man and his country. With the black man the need for assurance is understandable. The same argument could as reasonably be proffered in favor of the lover motif being used to suggest the relationship between a man and his God. "Ungauzed" "gaze" especially is remindful of the "bandage ready for your eyes" in "And Shall I Prime My Children, Pray, to Pray?" The image connotes eyes open to reality. The sestet helps to unravel some of the confusing ambiguity of the octave:

Surely—But I am very off from that.
From surely. From indeed. From the decent arrow
That was my clean naiveté and my faith.
This morning men deliver wounds and death.
They will deliver death and wounds tomorrow.
And I doubt all. You. Or a violet. (*World*, 57)

It is immediately obvious that "surely" has been used earlier as an expression of doubt instead of certainty. Doubt is not openly admitted about "the decent arrow" suggesting love, "clean naiveté and my faith" suggesting God, and the delivery of "wounds and death" suggesting war. "And I doubt all" clarifies the inverted meaning of "surely," and the persona's doubt about everything alluded to—lover, flag, God—becomes evident, making the ambiguity purposeful and meaningful.

Read negatively, the poem can plausibly be interpreted as social protest in perfect tune with the cynical tone of the other sonnets of this series. Surely the black man could never truthfully think of the country in terms of "mine"; surely the country has not been "all honest, lofty as a cloud" to him; surely the country would not assure him of its love; and surely the country's eyes are not open. However, beyond these meanings lies another layer of irony and ambiguity.

Because of the paradoxes inherent in American social duplicity, statements referring to them can often be simultaneously true and false, a prominent characteristic of the labyrinth. Ironically, for the black man it is true that conditions would remain as they were. The country to him would be as "lofty as a cloud" or as haughty. It is true that he should not be surprised or "awed," and there would be the "insolent" lip service to equal regard for all under the law. The most definite statement of the poem is that death and wounds will continue as before. It reinforces the ironic interpretation that stresses the continuation of things as they were.

In "Love Note II: Flag" the motif of the disillusionment of a soldier over unrequited love conveys the underlying social protest of the black man's disillusionment about the failure of his flag to champion his cause in his war for dignity. Miss Brooks alludes to the flag as a lady in the same kind of way she refers to democracy as a lady in "Negro Hero." The foxhole soldier is bitter about being whimsically jilted by the fair lady of democ-

racy whose flag he carries. The octave presents a sarcastic propo-
sition to the flag for help:

> Still, it is dear defiance now to carry
> Fair flags of you above my indignation,
> Top, with a pretty glory and a merry
> Softness, the scattered pound of my cold passion.
> I pull you down my foxhole. Do you mind:
> You burn in bits of saucy color then.
> I let you flutter out against the pained
> Volleys. Against my power crumpled and wan.

"Dear defiance" implies the indignation that some whites feel
when blacks invoke the protection promised by democracy. "Top,
with a pretty glory and merry softness" suggests the cheap,
superficial dressing on "cold passion." The soldier displays his
disgust by dragging the fair lady democracy into his fighting-
place, his "foxhole." "Do you mind" is a derisive question, for he
knows the abhorrence of the lady who would not voluntarily
visit him let alone champion his fight for dignity. "You burn in
bits of saucy color then" indicates democracy's indignation at the
invitation. The soldier lets democracy feel the attacks customary
to blacks in the ghetto and makes democracy know of his de-
bilitated condition with "power crumpled and wan." The sestet
helps to explain the labyrinthian duplicity of democracy by com-
paring it to the fickleness of a girl vacilating from love to repulsion like a fan blowing hot and cold:

> You, and the yellow pert exuberance
> of dandelion days, unmocking sun;
> The blowing of clear wind in your gay hair;
> Love changeful in you (like a music, or
> Like a sweet mournfulless, or like a dance,
> Or like the tender struggle of a fan). (World, 58)

In "The Progress" the war motif is used to convey a statement
about the naiveté of men. Men get so engrossed in their partisan
victories that they are momentarily blind to the larger defeat
suffered by all involved. The fear is expressed that wars will
occur again and again with no one winning in the larger sense.
Social protest from the perspective of the black man is not readily
apparent in this poem except to the extent that there is a strong

parallel between the persistent elusiveness of progress and peace in both world war and the black man's war for dignity. In both cases progress is often more apparent than real. The perplexed question near the end of the poem, "How shall we smile, congratulate; and how settle in chairs?" and the alarm at "the step of iron feet again" could apply as well to either war.

V   *"In the Mecca"*

By providing glimpses of a number of the occupants of a large, decaying apartment building teeming with representative types of people of the black ghetto, "In the Mecca" cuts across the various hells of the black experience and thereby contains elements of each of the dominant themes of Miss Brooks's poetry. While another major theme of the poem is spiritual death, the most central theme is the labyrinth. Imaginatively manipulating technique and content in order to evoke the labyrinth, the poet brings together seemingly unrelated or incongruous vignettes in a collage superimposed on a simple narrative background. Early in the poem Miss Brooks hints at the difficulty of seeing the common relationship of a number of diverse entities:

> When there were all those gods
> administering to panthers,
> jumping over mountains,
> and lighting stars and comets and a moon,
> what was their one Belief?
> what was their joining thing?

The question not only applies to the difficulty of deciphering the apparent hodge-podge of the poem but also reflects the real confusion that a person encounters in trying to arrange the various incidents of life into a meaningful whole. More specifically the passage suggests that in the black ghetto part of the labyrinthian effect is caused by everyone's having his own concept of god and/or devil, pursuing or fleeing it independently.

The literal search for the lost Pepita is symbolic of the characters' pursuits of the fulfillment of dreams of redemption. The search provides a background upon which these parts are presented.

Mrs. Sallie Smith, an old black work lady who lives in the large overcrowded ghetto apartment building called the "Mecca" on the south side of Chicago, comes home tired from church service, ascends the stairs to her fourth floor apartment and begins to help her oldest daughter prepare a meal. Eight of her nine children and Mrs. Sallie are shown to engage in reverie respectively appropriate to fulfill each of their particular needs and wants. When suddenly they realize that the youngest, Pepita, is missing, they search frantically through the Mecca and up and down the street. No one claims to have seen her, but each person consulted manages to reveal his own want or need that he is constantly searching for. The police come and little Pepita is found murdered under Jamaican Edward's cot. The many halts and reversal and dead ends in the presentation are themselves suggestive of the labyrinth. The reader is confused long enough to induce empathy for the desperately sane inhabitants of the Mecca.

The labyrinthian aspects of "In the Mecca" are particularly effected by the imagery. For instance, the name of the building, "Mecca," suggests yearnings for or pursuit of ideals. The idea of a holy city is not inappropriate here, for many of the pursuits are religious in nature as people attempt to reach beyond the limits of the misery of their natural worlds for solace in supernatural ones. The physical aspects of the building itself also represent the labyrinth. Halls, as in other poems, represent confusion while doors represent choices that for the people of her poetry usually lead to thwarting situations. For example, with a combination of door and hall imagery, the poet evokes a sense of confusion and frustration as Pepita's family vainly searches for her:

> In twos!
> In threes! Knock-knocking down the martyred halls
> at doors behind whose yelling oak or pine
>   many flowers start, choke, reach up,
>   want help, get it, do not get it,
>   rally, bloom, or die on the wasting vine.

In another instance the door is personified and asks questions which the family cannot answer:

> S. and eight of her children reach their door. The
> door says, "What are you doing here? and where
> is Pepita the puny—the halted, glad-sad child?"

> They pet themselves, subdue
> the legislation of their yoke and devils.

This passage shows that Pepita's family is projecting its own frustration and confusion into the environment.

Light and sight images are also pervasively used to suggest the importance of perception in plying the labyrinth. Very early in the poem as Mrs. Sallie returns from church service, her eye is referred to as "unrinsed," indicating that her perception was still affected by the service. In the passages that follow, the reader sees the world through the eyes of Mrs. Sallie. Her perception of her kitchen indicates her negative attitude:

> Now Mrs. Sallie
> confers her bird-hat to her kitchen table,
> and sees her kitchen. It is bad, is bad,
> her eyes say, and My soft antagonist,
> her eyes say, and My headlong tax and mote,
> her eyes say, and My maniac default,
> my least light.
> "But all my lights are little!"

This passage with its extensive use of light and sight images illustrates the low opinion she has of herself. The following passage expresses her sense of frustration about her thwarted condition and her "little lights" as well as her strange compulsion to continue to seek answers:

> Her denunciation
> slaps savagely not only this sick kitchen but
> her Lord's annulment of the main event.
> "I want to decorate!" but what is that? A
> pomade atop a sewage. An offense.
> First comes correctness, then embellishment!
> And music, mode, and mixed philosophy
> may follow fitly on propriety
> to tame the whiskey of our discontent!
> "What can I do?"
>   But World (a sheep)
> wants to be Told.
> If you ask a question, you
> can't stop there.
> You must keep going.

> You can't stop there: World will
> waive; will be
> facetious, angry. You can't stop there.
> You have to keep on going.

One chief pursuit of the tenants is redemptive relief from the present conditions. To help give the collage unity the poet employs Alfred, a tenant in the Mecca, to serve as a chorus does in tragedy by foreshadowing, summarizing, and interpreting the action as the characters pursue their separate wants and needs.[17] While many of the incidents involving the tenants deal with spiritual death, the comments of Alfred consistently interpret these incidents as labyrinthian. The diversity of interests and pursuits is foreshadowed by Alfred's question about what common belief joined those who in ancient times believed in a number of different gods. The eight children of Mrs. Sallie show that they have several different special characterizing dreams or yearnings in terms of fulfilling, replacing, or coping with what they consider to be the most important deficiencies of their lives. Yvonne finds redemption by daydreaming about love; Melodie Mary, by championing the cause of the lowly have-nots and oppressed including rats and roaches; Briggs, by forfeiting his identity to the gang of which he is a member; Tennessee, by remaining passive and uninvolved with the world; Thomas Earl, by pretending to be Johnny Appleseed; Emmet, Cap, and Casey, by eating "greens and hock of ham and a spoon of sweet potato." Mrs. Sallie first seeks rest at home from her life's battles, part of which is expressed by her thwarted wish to decorate. Frustrated, she asks, "What can I do?" and the lines following the question show a compulsion to run the maze. Mrs. Sallie also would be "Her Lady," apparently referring to the white woman for whom she works.

As if in answer to Alfred's question of how unity is achieved out of great diversity, the children and Mrs. Sallie all become concerned together about a common loss. When the searching Smiths ask Alfred whether or not he has seen Pepita, he answers negatively and gives a perfect description of the Mecca in terms of the labyrinth:

> No, Alfred has not seen Pepita Smith.
> But he (who might have been an architect)

> can speak of Mecca: firm arms surround
> disorders, bruising ruses and small hells,
> small semiheavens: hug barbarous rhetoric
> built of buzz, coma and petite pell-mells.

The many pursuits of the tenants bear out the notion that people will follow "many of a cloven foot" as predicted in "People Protest in Sprawling Lightless Ways." Many of the pursuits related to religion such as those associated with Prophet Williams, St. Julia, Aunt Dill, and with Mrs. Sallie herself indicate a groping for a solution to the labyrinth. When asked about Pepita's whereabouts, the tenants present a convincing picture of a key factor in the labyrinth—the extreme lack of concern for others.[18] The state of perpetual preoccupation with self virtually assures that every inquiry in the quest will meet with discouragement.

In summarizing the needs of those in the labyrinth, Alfred says:

> Not Baudelaire, Bob Browning, not Neruda.
> Giants over Steeples
> are wanted in this Crazy-eyes, this Scar.
> A violent reverse.
> We part from all we thought we knew of love
> and of dismay-with-flags-on. What we know
> is that there are confusion and conclusion.
> Rending.
> Even the hardest parting is a contribution. . .
> Farewell. And Hail! Until Farewell again.

This statement acknowledges the existence of, suggests the cause of, and offers a solution to this "crazy-eyes," this "confusion and conclusion" which comprise the labyrinth. The "violent reverse" he suggests is the same as that dealt with in "A Lovely Love," where traditionally positive values become negative, and vice versa. Alfred's final observation on the labyrinth in the Mecca is the most positive statement of the whole poem and points, though vaguely, toward rebirth:

> And steadily
> an essential sanity, black and electric
> builds to a reportage and redemption.

> A hot estrangement.
> A material collapse
> that is Construction. (*World*, 377–403)

This chapter has focused on Miss Brooks's treatment of the most characteristic condition of the black's hell—the psychological and sociological environments which give rise to the great confusion in the United States on matters concerning relations between black people and white people. Perhaps it is because much of the black man's environment is shaped to a great extent by the white man that Miss Brooks's poetry devotes some attention to the prejudices of the white man.

Attention is also paid, of course, to the part of the environment caused by the black's adjustment to the encompassing national schizophrenia. The poet portrays the black as constantly searching for seemingly unattainable goals, meeting repeated frustrations in his quest for such elusive prizes as peace of mind, sanity, dignity, and physical and psychological security for himself and his loved ones.

In the same way that physical death is used by the poet as a major image of spiritual death, the physical environment is used as an image of the psychological environment which is foisted on blacks by the social traditions of the United States. Both physical and psychological environments easily suggest a maze or labyrinth to be assailed or escaped by the black man. Miss Brooks's consistent reference to the physical aspects of the black ghetto in meaningful relation to the state of confusion of the black man clarifies the use of these images to suggest a labyrinthian situation. The implication is that if the black man traverses his mandatory route successfully, he will usher in a rebirth of glory for himself and the world. This point is alluded to in the last lines of "Men of Careful Turns, Haters of Forks in the Road."

> Rise.
> Let us combine. There are no magics or elves
> Or timely godmothers to guide us. We are lost, must
> Wizard a track through our own screaming weed. (*World*, 124)

CHAPTER 6

Survival

WHEREAS the previous chapter, "The Labyrinth," focuses on the various aspects of the blacks' social environment, this one focuses on Miss Brooks's treatment of the inner genius and strengths of the black as a person. Instead of an assessment of the hazards faced by the black in traversing a dangerous course, this chapter provides an account of the blacks' racial qualities, as they appear in Miss Brooks's poetry, that enable them to exist in their environment with some degree of success. In order to survive, blacks have had to maintain a precarious balance between restraint and militance while moving always toward their concept of rebirth of freedom. Restraint has been the prevailing approach used for the protection of the black's physical well-being, especially for the avoidance of physical death. Militance, on the other hand, has been the result of the black's occasional intolerance of the indignation he suffers and is necessary for the survival of his spirit which compels him toward a rebirth of freedom. The rebirth of freedom is a tacit dream that blacks have of someday fulfilling the reversal of the fall from former glory. As such it lends heroic significance to the restraint and militance experienced by black people.

Survival—even subconscious survival—is connected in Miss Brooks's poetry to a hope of returning to a former glory as expressed in "People Protest in Sprawling Lightless Ways," where the protestor learns early to abort his furies but still thinks of former glory and of returning to it. Otherwise, though the results are the same, the empahsis would be on spiritual death. Miss Brooks celebrates the black's intuitively ingenious harboring of life in death. Ironically, through their apparent abject weakness they have exhibited a great capacity for survival. The black has been hero while being lackey, buffon, and scapegoat. The poet asserts, especially in *In the Mecca* and *Riot*, that the black has

131

wrapped life delicately in the protective, disarming callus of death which becomes a seed pod that produces that harvest of the black's self-fulfillment.

The poet's idea of survival is also depicted as a transporting of the black's spiritual life through a period of death from which it emerges intact to flourish in a more healthful environment. "First Fight. Then Fiddle," for instance, points out the necessity of militance to preserve a place where the spirit can flourish, and "My Dreams, My Works, Must Wait till after Hell" stresses the importance of spiritually being able to ·enjoy freedom if it comes. There are those, however, whose constitutions will not allow payment of such a high price for physical life and the gestation-survival of the human spirit. Instead the spirit flowers into glorious adulthood and springs out of its bonds, as in "Medgar Evers" and "Malcolm X" and with many other nonfictional people such as Martin Luther King, Eldridge Cleaver, Adam Clayton Powell, Jr., Muhammad Ali, H. Rapp Brown, Stokely Carmichael, the Black Panthers, the Soledad Brothers, Angela Davis, Nat Turner, Denmark Vesey, and so forth. Almost invariably the militants die or are rendered impotent by the retaliation of a hostile environment. "The Ballad of Rudolph Reed" uses a fictional character to dramatize restraint being pushed too far and exploding into militance.

Paradoxically even these dead effect a sacrificial preservation of the spirit. The spirit being protected is not a peculiarly black spirit; it is the *human spirit* in blacks, manifested in ways that reflect the black experience. The sacrifice is a clear reminder to the psyches of black people that the spirit of life dwells in them as "a wild inflammable stuff" "at the root of the will," and the old hope of restoration of glory is renewed. It says that black people are proud and strong and brave. The black feasts on this heroic sacrifice even as he cries, for it is part of his sustenance and his source of resilience.

As if to emphasize the spiritual nature of the black's rebirth, Miss Brooks alludes to it often in terms of redemption, the second coming of Christ, or other religious phenomena. The black man, like Christ, has borne the cross of persecution largely for being what he is. In the United States he has been the only true embodiment of the melting-pot myth, embracing all kinds of people from the nine-tenths white Adam Clayton Powells to the ten-tenths black Stokely Carmichaels.

The universality of rebirth is implied by the association with the fulfillment of the idea of democracy. Rebirth will be redemptive and corrective of a general evil perpetrated on both blacks and whites. Miss Brooks implies that whites cannot be free themselves until they stop holding blacks in bondage. "A Bronzeville Mother Loiters in Mississippi. Meanwhile, a Mississippi Mother Burns Bacon," for example, illustrates the kind of bondage the white man places on himself in order to restrict the freedom of the black man. Therefore, rebirth does not refer only to the blacks' reclamation of freedom but also to the salvation they will bring to mankind in general.

I   *Restraint: First Step to Rebirth*

The first and most basic step toward spiritual rebirth and ultimate survival is restraint, which ingeniously uses death as a seed pod to harbor physical and spiritual life. Miss Brooks's poetry depicts people who employ restraint by engaging in a number of diversions that camouflage or justify the blacks' acquiescence to their oppressors. The diversions most often take the form of false goals or consolations that ease the pain of the unachieved goal of freedom.

Very often these diversions from the realities of life are succinctly hinted at by Miss Brooks's technique of using contrasting terms within a phrase with the negative term undermining the effect of the positive one. The positive term represents a diversion and the negative term represents a more comprehensive corresponding reality. "Flowers upon rot" in "The Funeral," for instance, shows the solace that the flowers are supposed to bring betrayed by their association with "rot," representing death:

> Sick
> Thick odor-loveliness winds nicely about the
>   shape of mourning,
> A dainty horror. People think of flowers upon rot—
> And for moments together the corpse is no colder
>   than they

"Dainty horror," another set of contrasting terms, describes the essence of the funeral and also sets an example for the mechanism of Miss Brooks's use of the oxymoron and other forms of

contrasting terms to reveal the clever ruse employed by black
people in order to remain blind toward certain realities and
thereby be effectively restrained from assuming responsibility for
them. This interpretation of the use of contrasting terms is borne
out by a consistent pattern maintained in a number of other
poems. Later in "The Funeral" the reference to willful blindness is clear: "Preacher and tradition of piety and propriety rise.
The people wait/For the dear blindfold" (*World*, 10). A similar
strategy for restraint is used in "The Sundays of Satin-Legs
Smith." Here Miss Brooks suggests in six lines an idea that is
repeated and embellished throughout the poem—that Satin-Legs
creates a role of unlikely grandeur for himself and proceeds to
perform for his own benefit:

> He waits a moment, he designs his reign,
> That no performance may be plain or vain.
> Then rises in a clear delirium.
>
> He sheds, with his pajamas, shabby days,
> And his desertedness, his intricate fear, the
> Postponed resentments and the prim precautions. (*World*, 26)

The oxymoron "clear delirium" indicates that while his fantasy
has internal clarity, it is not aligned with the real world. "De-
signs his reign" and "performance" suggest a preparation to "act"
the part of some grand person. That this role is a deception is
indicated by his attempt to shed his "shabby days." Most important is that he avoids the heavy responsibilities of life, "his intricate fear" of facing the white man and of facing himself as a
coward. By eliminating the "postponed resentments and the prim
precautions" from his fantasized world, he effectively restrains
or redirects his aggressions in order to survive with little danger
of becoming militant or even conspicuous. It is significant that
he chooses an object of his redirected aggression which can compensate for his apparent lack of virility in the larger scheme of
things.

The feminine loveliness of Mary Ann, a Rangerette in "Gang
Girls," described as "a rose in a whiskey glass," is negated by the
severe restraint she must practice:

> Mary Ann
> uses the nutrients of her orient,

> but sometimes sighs for Cities of blue and jewel
> beyond her Ranger rim of Cottage Grove.
> (Bowery Boys, Disciples, Whip-Birds will
> dissolve no margins, stop no savory sanctities.)

She, like Satin-Legs, tries to compensate for her loneliness and
necessary restraint by making love central in her life:

> Love's another departure.
> Will there be any arrivals, confirmations?
> Will there be gleaning?
>
> Mary, the Shakedancer's child
> from the rooming-flat, pants carefully, peers at
> her laboring lover. . .
>   Mary! Mary Ann!
> Settle for sandwiches! settle for stocking caps!
> for sudden blood, aborted carnival,
> the props and niceties of non-loneliness—
> the rhymes of Leaning. (*World*, 420)

The capitalized word, "Leaning," is an indication that survival is
involved, for in Miss Brooks's poetry the imagery of leaning
usually suggests a transcendence of a very negative period or
condition. To Mary love is another departure from reality and
sweetens the sourness of her deprivation.

Mrs. Sallie in "In the Mecca" realizes that her desired diversion is only a camouflage of her real frustration. After coming
home tired, she views her kitchen with disgust and at first expresses her displeasure at not being able to decorate:

> Her denunciation
> saps savagely not only this sick kitchen but
> her Lord's annulment of the main event.
> "I want to decorate!"

Then she immediately realizes that the diversion of decorating
would be absurdly hollow:

> But what is that: A
> pomade atop a sewage. An offense.
>
> First comes correctness, then embellishment!
> And music, mode, and mixed philosophy

> may follow fitly on propriety
> to tame the whiskey of our discontent!

"A pomade atop a sewage" is another example of Miss Brooks's use of contrasting terms to suggest survival through restraint. "Pomade" alludes to the momentary diversion and "sewage" wrenches Mrs. Sallie and the reader back to the reality of her situation. Mrs. Sallie, who is variously referred to by such phrases as "the eye unrinsed" and "her stretched eyes" and through whose eyes much of the poem is seen, sees what many characters of Miss Brooks never face—that correctness should come before embellishment. She reiterates the theme of "First Fight. Then Fiddle" as she allows herself a fleeting glimpse of reality. Mrs. Sallie implies that "music, mode, and mixed philosophy" will be appropriate to restrain the harshness of black people's discontent only after corrections are made of the oppressive social conditions in the United States. "Whiskey" generalizes the myriad diversions from these conditions. The abrupt switch from a reference to the first-person-singlar pronouns to "our" when referring to discontent is a hint that the passage applies to black people in general rather than to Mrs. Sallie in particular. By opening her eyes, she faces the terrible labyrinth that was the subject of Chapter 5. Her perplexed question and her own resolution illustrate that her concern at this point is with survival:

> "What can I do?"
>   But World (a sheep)
> wants to be Told.
> If you ask a question, you
> can't stop there.
> You must keep going.
> You can't stop there: World will
> Waive, will be
> facetious, angry. You can't stop there.
> You have to keep on going.

She is conscious about the reaction of the world to her question which looks for an alternative to restraining or "taming" of our discontent. Getting as far as the question, she realizes that without answers she must simply "keep on going," restraining herself as best she can for survival.

A very similar use of imagery, situation, and contrasting terms occurs later in "In the Mecca" to depict the result of Marian's fight to keep violent reaction from overpowering restraint. She too is disgusted with her physical surroundings and overall situation:

> At iron: at ire with faucet, husband, young.
> Knows no
> gold hour
> slings
> but sparsely, and subscribes to axioms
> atop her gargoyles and tamed foam. Good axioms.

"Axioms atop her gargoyles" illustrates her ploy to control the "foam" of her ire. It is apparent that the restraining effect of axioms is not sufficient. She, like Mrs. Sallie, wants to create. Marian's desired diversion is somewhat more bizarre than is Mrs. Sallie's:

> Craves crime: her murder, her deep wounding, or
>   a leprosy so lovely as to pop
> the slights and sleep of her community,
> her Mecca. (*World*, 377–403)

Fulfillment of Marian's desire would be a capitulation to the oppression of her situation and a veering away from survival toward masochism.[1] There is no indication, however, that she like Mrs. Sallie does not "keep on going."

Similarly, the old yellow pair in "The Bean Eaters" "keep on putting on their clothes and putting things away" as they hang on to their lives in their drab rented apartment subsisting largely on beans. It is implied that memory is one of the main contributors to their survival:

> And remembering. . .
> Remembering, with twinklings and twinges,
> As they lean over the beans in their rented back
>   room that
>   is full of beads and receipts and dolls and
>   cloths,
>   tobacco crumbs, vases and fringes. (*World*, 314)

Again Miss Brooks uses the image of "leaning" to suggest a transcendence of a period of trouble. The leaning suggests not only their own survival but also has broader application to the survival of the black man. The list of trinkets is very like a list of items used to buy slaves in Africa [2] and therefore suggests that the example of the plodding, remembering survival of this old yellow pair is the heart of the survival of black men everywhere.

Chapter 4 on "The Fall from Glory" points out Miss Brooks's frequent implication that the black man's racial memory of the fall from glory can act as an adjunct to survival by prompting restraint and patience when they are needed. "The Sundays of Satin-Legs Smith" is appropriate for discussion of the black man's memory, not because it depicts a remembrance of glory, royalty, or even of better times, but because it illustrates very plainly Miss Brooks's awareness of the pervasiveness and effectiveness of certain subconscious memories which have evolved as a matter of survival. Throughout the poem the persona engages the addressee and the reader in speculation about the influences that have shaped Satin-Legs's tastes in bath oils, clothes, music, food, and women. Repeatedly when the addressee seems to expect Satin-Legs's choices to be "in the best of taste and straight tradition," the persona reminds the addressee that Satin-Legs's

> heritage of cabbage and pigtails,
> Old intimacy with alleys, garbage pails,
> Down in the deep (but always beautiful) South
> Where roses blush their blithest (it is said)
> And sweet magnolias put Chanel to shame

prevails too strongly upon him to make other kinds of choices. The strength of this heritage is concisely summarized in these lines:

> The pasts of his ancestors lean against
> Him. Crowd him. Fog out his identity.
> Hundreds of hungers mingle with his own,
> Hundreds of voices advise so dexterously
> He quite considers his reactions his,
> Judges he walks most powerfully alone,
> That everything is—simply what it is. (*World*, 27, 30)

This statement illustrates beyond Satin-Legs's heritage in particular the influence of the black experience on black people.

Once again the term "lean" clearly connotes a transcendence, a deftly subtle survival of the black man.

The influence of tradition on restraint is an important part of "Men of Careful Turn, Haters of Forks in the Road." The poem shows the black appealing to whites for an equal sharing of their mutual estate. American social tradition is cast as an intimidating restrainer of the black suppliant who makes an analogy in which he denounces his role as a woman warily loving a drunken mate.

> And to love you
> No more as a woman loves a drunken mate,
> Restraining full caress and good my Dear,
> Even pity for the heaviness and the need—
> Fearing sudden fire out of the uncaring mouth,
> Boiling in the slack eyes, and the traditional blow.
> Next, the indifference formal, deep and slow. (*World*, 123)

This analogy is very much like the one in "Negro Hero" where Democracy is referred to as "my fair lady":

> Their white-gowned democracy was my fair lady.
> With her knife lying cold, straight, in the softness
>   of her sweet-flowing sleeve.
>
> But for the sake of her dear smiling mouth and the
>   stuttered promise I toyed with my life.
> I threw back!—I would not remember
> Entirely the knife. (*World*, 33)

In "Men of Careful Turns, Haters of Forks in the Road" American tradition warns the suppliant to

> Remember
> When cruelty, metal, public, uncomplex,
> Trampled you obviously and every hour. . .
> . . . .
> And the report is
> What's old is wise, At any rate, the line is
> Long and electric. Lean beyond and nod.
> Be sprightly. Wave. Extend your hand and teeth.
> But never forget it stretches there beneath. (*World*, 123–24)

The suppliant is advised to restrain his transcendence (suggested here by "lean") across perilous conditions for the sake of survival.

The suppliant counters, however, with advice of his own that they must work together to solve their common problems.

II *The Role of Religion in Survival*

As part of the traditions that influence the black man toward restraint, religion plays an important role. Miss Brooks in "And Shall I Prime My Children, Pray, to Pray?" alludes to the general restraining effect of religion. The persona is pondering the worthwhileness of having his children ascribe to religion as an absolute to help them endure the world. It is realized, however, that in order for the children to achieve the desired assurance, a willing suspension of disbelief will be necessary. Thought of this requirement is expressed in negative terms revealing the persona's cynical tone: "Children, confine your lights in jellied rules; resemble graves; be metaphysical mules. . . ." "Confine your lights" refers to the advice to curb healthy curiosity and reliance upon proof, and "in jellied rules" connotes that the medicine of the rules will be sweetened by the ultimate rewards of blindness to reality. Even more cynicism is implied in the use of "graves" to equate religion with death and of "metaphysical mules" to equate it with the toil of explaining worldly phenomena and occurrences, particularly of the black experience, in religious terms. Here again, in spite of the cynicism, the parent is ready to use religion to help his children survive with some assurance of the worthiness of their place in the scheme of things:

> Behind the scurryings of your neat motif
> I shall wait, if you wish: revise the psalm
> If that should frighten you: sew up belief
> If that should tear: turn, singularly calm
> At forehead and at fingers rather wise,
> Holding and bandage ready for your eyes. (*World*, 101)

Not only would the children be encouraged to restrain their natural skepticism but also the parent would restrain his cynicism in order to help his children survive.

The importance of religion as a device to effect survival through restraint is clearly demonstrated in "In the Mecca." While not all the examples of restraint in this poem are directly religious in nature, most of them have religious overtones. The first of many instances of restraint is afforded by the descriptions of Mrs. Sallie's frame of mind as she arrives at her home in the Mecca apartment building:

> S. Smith is Mrs. Sallie. Mrs. Sallie
> hies home to Mecca, hies to marvelous rest;
> ascends the sick and influential stair.
> The eye unrinsed, the mouth absurd
> with the last sourings of the master's Feast.
> She plans
> to set severity apart,
> to unclench the heavy folly of the fist.
> Infirm booms
> and suns that have not spoken die behind this
> low-brown butterball. Our prudent partridge.
> A fragmentary attar and armed coma.
> A fugitive attar and a district hymn.

Miss Brooks, by referring to the "unrinsed eye" and the remnants from the "master's Feast" still tasted, makes an allusion to the celebration of the Eucharist and indicates that Mrs. Sallie's perception is still influenced by the religious service. Religion is here a mollifier because she will no longer be severe and associates the fist with heavy folly. With her explosive instincts subdued she cautiously chooses not to fight. Recognizing her weakness described as "infirm booms and suns that have not spoken," she is prudent to compromise with her oppressor and thereby remove herself from danger. "Our" at first may seem a casual use, but it alludes to the collective protective posture of black parents, particularly mothers. "Partridge" also evokes protective motherhood. If as she implies elsewhere only people who have no children can be hard, the fact that she has nine perhaps explains her choice.

"Fragmentary attar" suggests that her womanly essence is incomplete while "armed coma" refers to latent subdued explosiveness. "Fugitive attar" implies more strongly that her burden of being protector-provider has relegated her role as sex-love object for males to a relatively unimportant position. "District hymn" refers to her being a song of praise to the master by her prudent acquiescence to his will. "District" gives the hymn a definite earthly tie limiting the application of the hymn and therefore betrays the fact that the real allegiance is in effect to the white lord. The "master's Feast" alludes to Holy Communion but is perhaps also a reference to the dinner at the earthly master's (not capitalized) house where she works. She brings home gleanings from the earthly master's feast for her children. The comparison of the two masters suggests that while acquiescence to an earthly master is demeaning and sometimes intolerable, acquiescence to the heavenly master can be very gratifying and fulfilling. Ascription to the teachings of Jesus has lightened the black man's burden of submission to the white man by sanctifying his acts of restraint that would otherwise be degrading. By figuratively equating the earthly and heavenly masters, Miss Brooks has used artful ambiguity to reveal a basic and intricate rationale for the black man's use of religion as an instrument of survival through restraint.

St. Julia exemplifies a more indirect kind of restraint as she lavishly praises the "Lord" in terms simultaneously showing a great deal of familiarity and evoking the comforting benefactor of the "Twenty-third Psalm":

> Sees old St. Julia Jones, who has had prayer,
> and who is rising from amenable knees
> inside the wide-flung door of 215.
> "Isn't He wonderfulwonderful!" cries St. Julia.
> "Isn't our Lord the greatest to the brim?
> The light of my life. And I lie late
> past the still pastures. And meadows. He's the comfort
> and wine and piccalilli for my soul.
> He hunts me up the coffee for my cup.
> O how I love that Lord."

This mixture of intimate familiarity with Old Testament remoteness extends more subtly the ambiguous reference to the earthly and heavenly masters. Religion is shown here to be capable not only of mollifying one's despair, but also of glorifying one's deprived conditions. It causes St. Julia to count her blessings which are more acceptable if attributed to the benevolence of the heavenly Lord than if recognized to be the residue or gleanings from the booty of landlords and other earthly rulers. By seeing the Lord as their vanguard, Mrs. Sallie grudgingly and St. Julia euphorically accepted the conveniently docile roles prescribed to them by religion.

Prophet Williams also diverts his aggression into religious

involvement; however, instead of simply using religion to ease the acceptance of exploitation, he uses it also to exploit others who use it to ease their acceptance of exploitation and oppression. His inclination to exploit and his restraint of his power and explosiveness are implied concisely in the following brief description:

> Speaks
> to Prophet Williams, young beyond St. Julia,
> and rich with Bible, pimples, pout; who reeks
> with lust for his disciple, is an engine
> of candid steel hugging combustibles.

In contrast to St. Julia's laudatory allusion to the Lord in terms of the "Twenty-third Psalm," Loam Norton alludes sardonically to the "Twenty-third Psalm" to express his disdain for the Lord's protection:

> Although he has not seen Pepita, Loam
> Norton considers Belsen and Dachau,
> regrets all old unkindnesses and harms.
> . . . The Lord was their shepherd.
> Yet did they want.
> Joyfully would they have lain in jungles or pastures,
> walked besides waters. Their gaunt
> souls were not restored, their souls were banished.
> In the shadow valley
> They feared the evil, whether with or without God.
> They were comforted by no Rod,
> no Staff, but flayed by, O besieged by, shot a-plenty.
> The prepared table was the rot or curd of the day.
> Anointings were of lice. Blood was the spillage of cups.
> Goodness and mercy should follow them
>   all the days of their death.
> They should dwell in the house of the Lord forever
> and, dwelling, save a place for me.
> I am not remote,
> not unconcerned. . . . (*World*, 377–88)

He laments the extermination of Jews at Belsen and Dachau and scoffs at the use of religion as a restrainer because the Jews believed and were still vanquished. The idea that one should waive his responsibility to protect himself in favor of reliance upon the apparently "remote" and "unconcerned" Lord is ridiculed and shown to be dangerous. The last four lines of the above passage imply that one's fellow man is one's best source of protection, for Loam states that he is neither "remote nor unconcerned" as he presumes the Lord to be.

III   *Redemption through Death*

It has been pointed out that religion affords some black men a kind of vicarious obeisance to the white man through obeisance to God. For this reason restraint connected with religion is justified on the basis of compensation to be made in the next world. For other black men, however, the rewards of restraint are much more mundane whether the restraint be inspired or nourished by diversion, memory, tradition, or religion. Some cannot endure the pain of submission for the sake of physical survival. For these dying itself can be redemptive and therefore conducive to a militance that testifies to the intactness of the latent human spirit in all black men.

Miss Brooks's "The Ballad of Rudolph Reed" exemplifies the human spirit swelling out of its bonds and exulting briefly before Rudolph is killed. Rudolph Reed, described as "oaken" (meaning tough), is mainly concerned with the physical safety of his family when he initially refuses to answer the violence of his neighbors after moving with his family into a previously all-white neighborhood. The effort he makes to restrain himself from responding in kind to the violence is clear:

> The first night, a rock, big as two fists.
> The second, a rock big as three.
> But nary a curse cursed Rudolph Reed.
> (Though oaken as man could be.)
>
> The third night, a silvery ring of glass.
> Patience ached to endure.
> But he looked, and lo! small Mabel's blood
> Was staining her gaze so pure.

The fact that he does not curse in spite of his oakenness suggests that he is making a great effort to refrain from violence. "Patience ached to endure" indicates his great effort at restraint for sake of survival. The word "but," however, hints that the sight of "small Mabel's blood" makes it intolerable for him not to respond with violence:

> Then up did rise our Rudolph Reed
> And pressed the hand of his wife,
> And went to the door with a thirty-four
> And a beastly butcher knife.
>
> He ran like a mad thing into the night
> And the words in his mouth were stinking.
> By the time he had hurt his first white man
> He was no longer thinking.
>
> By the time he had hurt his fourth white man
> Rudolph Reed was dead.

Rudolph Reed is a black prototype, as suggested by the word "our," yet he is bigger than most black men, as indicated earlier in the poem: "oakener than others in the nation."

Rudolph obviously chooses physical death over the spiritual death which he would have deserved had he not fought back. Furthermore, he sows the seeds of oakenness, for his children (who already "oakened as they grew") will emulate his spirit of militance in the face of overbearing oppression, rather than continued submission. The deliberate pressing of his wife's hand implies that they both know that he must do as he does. She too meets her responsibility to the survival of the spirit as she resolutely continues with performance of the necessities of life: "Her oak-eyed mother did no thing/But change the bloody gauze" (*World*, 362). Here her stoic oakenness sets the correct example for her children and pays the highest compliment to her martyred husband while she simultaneously restrains herself from acts of violent retribution.

Miss Brooks's treatment of the black man's simultaneous sustaining of physical and spiritual life by maintaining a fine balance between restraint and militance has been demonstrated in "The Ballad of Rudolph Reed" and "In the Mecca." "Riders to the Blood-Red Wrath" deals even more thoroughly with the theme of survival by the skillful managing of internal and external forces capable of bringing death. Against the background of the freedom rides of the early 1960s the poem depicts a black man commenting on his present state of dilemma and paradox be-

tween restraint and militance and contemplating the glory of
rebirth. He recognizes that he is a hero while being prudent
simply because he has "deftly" "endured" among callous and
warlike white oppressors. The hero also realizes the blindness
and deafness of the whites to the suffering of the blacks.

The poem begins with the hero's observation that his deft
survival has escaped the whites:

> My proper prudence toward his proper probe
> Astonished their ancestral seemliness.
> It was a not-nice risk a wrought risk, was
> An indelicate risk, they thought. And an excess.
> Howas I handled my discordances
> And prides and apoplectic ice, howas
> I reined my charger, channeled the fit fume
> Of his most splendid honorable jazz
> Escaped the closing the averted sight
> Waiving all witness except of rotted flowers
> Framed in maimed velvet. That mad demi-art
> Of ancient and irrevocable hours.
> Waiving all witness except of dimnesses
> From which extrude beloved and pennant arms
> Of a renegade death impatient at his shrine
> And keen to share the gases of his charms
> They veer to vintage. Careening from tomorrows.
> Blaring away from my just genesis.
> They loot Last Night. They hug old graves, root up
> Decomposition, warm it with a kiss.

"Proper prudence" as a reference to the accommodations that are
made necessary by survival is similar to the "prudent partridge"
used to describe Mrs. Sallie in "In the Mecca." It signifies a cau-
tion appropriate to the danger in the situation. The handling of
his discordances, the reining of his charger, and the channeling
of his fit fume refer to the struggle of the black man to control,
without killing, his militance, for it is alive, splendid and honorable but in danger of death.

"Closing and averted" suggests that the blindness is a willful
refusal to see rather than inability to see on the part of the white
man. The white man here is associated with death, as evoked by
"rotted flowers," "maimed velvet," "renegade death," "old graves,"
and "decomposition" and with war, as hinted at by "pennant
arms."

The hints of war appearing in the first section of the poem are confirmed and intensified in the second. The war is no longer general and is no longer associated with the white man directly but to the struggle within the black man:

> The National Anthem vampires at the blood.
> I am a uniform. Not brusque. I bray
> Through blur and blunder in a little voice!
> This is a tender grandeur, a tied fray!
> Under macabres, strategem and fair
> Fine smiles upon the face of holocaust,
> My scream! unedited, unfrivolous.
> My laboring unlatched braid of heat and frost.
> I hurt, I keep that scream in at what pain:
> At what repeal of salvage and eclipse
> Army unhonored, meriting the gold, I
> Have sewn my guns inside my burning lips.

In this passage the white man's deafness to the "bray" and "scream" of the black man complements his blindness to the black man's tactful ploy of survival shown in the first passage. Again the deftness escapes the whites as the black man continues the restraint of his militance. In revealing this restraint this passage also affords another example of Miss Brooks's technique of showing restraint by juxtaposing two contrasting or seemingly incongruous terms. "A tied fray," "under macabres, strategem," "fair fine smiles upon the face of holocaust," and "braid of heat and frost" heighten the sense of tension from the opposing forces both operating within the black man to fulfill aspects of survival. The intense internal "war" is waged at great pain to the black man, who himself identifies with and becomes involved in this war simply by being what he is—black. Therefore, Miss Brooks's metaphor, "I am a uniform," is especially appropriate and hints at the heroism of those blacks who survive. In the last two lines of this section the hero of this poem pays eloquent tribute to the restraining "army" that has been largely responsible for effecting the black man's physical survival: "Army unhonored, meriting the gold, I/Have sewn my guns inside my burning lips." In the third section the hero is still concerned with the white man's detection of his secret war with the white man and within himself when he asks, "Did they detect my parley and replies?" The two aspects of the black man, restraint and militance, are

viewed as twins. In the first section the spirit of militance is
referred to as "charger" with "fit fume" and "splendid honorable
jazz." Here restraint is referred to as the "mare, the she thing,"
twin of the hero's revolution. The implication is that the less than
manly behavior of the black man has made his survival possible
by "lulling off men" and bending in supple submission to the
enemy.

In the next section the hero speaks with pride about his deft
endurance that has escaped the blind eyes and deaf ears of the
white man:

> They do not see how deftly I endure.
> Deep down the whirlwind of good rage I store
> Commemorations in an utter thrall.
> Although I need not eat them any more.

The hero applauds himself and the black man in general for his
ability to find relief from pain of his own rage through consoling
"commemorations" which he stores "in an utter thrall." These
commemorations refer to his proud racial memory of the black
experience. The next four sections deal with the hero's memories
of the glory and the freedom of Africa, the experience of the
slave trade, and slavery itself. From these memories he draws his
strength to endure. Furthermore, he uses the experience to im-
prove his own perspective and sensitivities, as indicated in these
lines:

> But my detention and my massive stain,
> And my distortion and my calvary
> I grind into a little light lorgnette
> Most sly: to read man's inhumanity,
> And I remark my Matter is not all.
> Man's chopped in China, in India indented.
> From Israel what's Arab is resented
> Europe candies custody and war.

While the memories sustain and console him, he is also proud of
the positive effects of his "detention and . . . massive stain."
These effects also help give him the resilience he needs not only
to survive, but also to lead the black man and the world in a
spiritual rebirth.

His broadened perspective and sensitivities enable him to see himself as an emissary of salvation:

> Behind my exposé
> I formalize my pity: "I shall cite,
> Star, and esteem all that which is of woman,
> Human and hardly human."
>
> Democracy and Christianity
> Recommence with me.

Conceiving of himself as an agent of the salvation of mankind from the inhumanity of the world as well as an agent of spiritual rebirth promotes restraint as well as impatience and eventual militance. The last lines of the poem conclude by referring to survival and hinting that militant struggle may be necessary to bring it about:

> And I ride ride I ride on to the end—
> Where glowers my continuing Calvary.
> I,
> My fellows, and those canny consorts of
> Our spread hands in this contretemps-for-love
> Ride into wrath, wraith and menagerie
>
> To fail, to flourish, to wither or to win.
> We lurch, distribute, we extend, begin. (*SP*, 115–18)

"And I ride ride I ride on to the end" suggests that the hero is going to continue to restrain himself until he rides into the "wrath, wraith and menagerie," which suggests militance and portends possible death for the charger and the mare. The outcome is uncertain: "To fail, to flourish, to wither or to win." But the conflict is inevitable: "We lurch, distribute, we extend, begin."

The rather conciliatory tone at the end of "Riders to the Blood-Red Wrath" is similar to the tone of "First Fight. Then Fiddle," where utopian harmony is an ultimate goal but can be achieved only through fighting to "civilize a space" in which to live. In both poems the black man sees himself as a savior of civilization. The idea of the black man taking matters of salvation into his own hands is briefly hinted at in " 'God Works in a Mysterious

Way.'" After a general expression of mounting skepticism and disenchantment the black man issues God an ultimatum to "Step forth in splendor, mortify our wolves/Or we assume a sovereignty ourselves." The break from the dependence on God is one of the initial steps toward militance, for it strips away a major restrainer of the expression of rage.

IV   *The Rise of Militance*

The militance illustrated in "The Ballad of Rudolph Reed" and "Riders to the Blood-Red Wrath" represents the basic spark stored or locked in the black man. "Malcolm X" reveals an opener—a key. So strongly is Malcolm X identified with militance that Miss Brooks is able to evoke the theme easily in the poem without making a concrete reference to militance.[3] But lines like

> We gasped. We saw the maleness.
> the maleness raking out and making guttural the air
> and pushing us to wall.
> . . . .
> He opened us—
> Who was a key,
>
> Who was a man (*World*, 411)

imply that he made it more difficult for the black man to fulfill his concept of manhood by continuing to lock his commemorations in "an utter thrall." Instead the black man is inspired to release his heretofore sustaining commemorations in the same way he is tempted to depend less on God and become more manly militant.

"The Wall" is a poem about the celebration of the Wall of Respect, the side wall of a typical ghetto tenement building in Chicago on the cornrer of 43rd and Langley on which is painted a mural depicting black heroes and black pride. Miss Brooks describes the black people gathered for the festival as "black furnaces":

> On Forty-third and Langley
> black furnaces resent ancient
> legislatures
> of ploy and scruple and practical gelatin.

> They keep the fever in,
> fondle the fever.
>
> All
> Worship the Wall. (*World*, 415)

This brief passage offers an example of the black man's break with tradition and its restrictions.

The black man's disenchantment with the inadequacies of religion and memory and his resentment of tradition indicate a movement away from the basic devices of restraint. The recourse seems to be militance. This is precisely the conclusion reached by Amos in "In the Mecca" as he reflects on the failure of the alternatives:

> "Takes time," granted the gradualist.
> "Starting from when?" asked Amos.
> Amos (not Alfred) says,
> "Shall we sit on ourselves; shall we wait behind
>   roses and veils
> for monsters to maul us,
>   for bulls to come butt us forever and ever,
> shall we scratch in our blood,
>   point air-powered hands at our wounds,
> reflect on the aims of our bulls?" And Amos
> (not Alfred) prays, for America prays
> "Bathe her in her beautiful blood.
> A long blood bath will wash her pure.
> Her skin needs special care.
> Let this good rage continue out beyond
> her power to believe or to surmise.
> Slap the false sweetness from that face.
> Great-nailed boots
> must kick her prostrate, heel-grind that soft breast,
> outrage her saucy pride,
> remove her fair fine mask.
> Let her lie there, panting and wild, her pain
> red, running roughly through the illustrious ruin—
> with nothing to do but think, think
> of how she was so long grand,
> flogging her dark one with her own hand,
> watching in meek amusement while he bled.
> Then shall she rise, recover.
> Never to forget." (*World*, 394–95)

Amos's prescription for a sick Democracy is to have it purged by blood and his tone suggests retribution as well as correction. Here again Miss Brooks indicates that the militance is mainly a means to bringing about a lasting harmony between blacks and whites in the United States.[4]

For Way-out Morgan, however, the militance is less constructive, almost totally retributive. He is so singleminded, in fact, that he hardly ever eats:

> He is not hungry, ever, though sinfully lean.
> He flourishes, ever, on porridge or pat of bean
> pudding or wiener sour—fills fearsomely
> on visions of Death-to-the-Hordes-of-the-White-Men!
> Death! (*World*, 400)

He "feasts" on the memories of atrocities committed against blacks and the just retaliation upon white men. His militance also progresses from the theory stage completely to the point where at least he is collecting guns, presumably with some plan of action in mind.

Way-out Morgan is contemplating a time of destruction for the white man like that represented in "Riot." The inscription at the beginning of the poem attributed to Martin Luther King states, "A riot is the language of the unheard." The brief picture of a riot is presented through the eyes of an upper-class white man, John Cabot, whose economic remoteness from and social disdain for the blacks bespeak the deaf ear that whites in general present to the screams or "bray" of the blacks. The items that Cabot is accustomed to such as his Jaguar, Grantully, Richard Gray and Distelheim, Masim's and Maison Henri are sufficient indicators of his wealth. That he nearly forgets these items "because the Negroes were coming down the street" is a clue to the extreme social distance between him and the Negroes. Furthermore, they were the poorest, roughest, loudest, and most indiscreet of Negroes—"(not like Two Dainty Negroes in Winnetka)"—and therefore all the more repulsive to Cabot. At one point Cabot whispered a prayer, "Don't let it touch me! the blackness! Lord!" But the Negroes touched, maligned, and mocked him, and "in a thrilling announcement" cried: "Cabot! John! You are a desperate man/and the desperate die expensively today." When John Cabot dies among "the smoke and fire and broken glass and blood," he condescended by magnanimously paraphrasing Jesus's dying prayer:

> "Lord!
> Forgive these nigguhs that know not what
> they do." (*Riot*, 9–10)[5]

This paraphrase, along with John Cabot's having the same initials as Jesus Christ, suggest that Miss Brooks joins the black in mocking Cabot. The "thrilling announcement" and the "terrific touch" are partial fulfillments of the black man's wish for retribution and correction.

In "To Keorapetse Kgositsile (Willie)" the motivation for militance is less retribution than it is a recognition that it is essential to physical as well as spiritual survival. Using his keen perception, Willie ascertains the horror of the spiritual and physical danger the black man is in. The spiritual danger is portrayed in these lines:

> Look! Look to *this* page!
> A horror here
> walks toward you in working clothes.
>   He sees
> hellishness among the half-men.
> He sees
> pellmelling loneliness in the
> center of grouphood
> He sees
> lenient dignity. He
> sees pretty flowers under blood.

The picture is drawn with the aid of contrasting terms which emphasize the confusion and the impropriety of the situation. "Hellishness" refers to the death of the spirit which renders men only "half-men." The general apathetic stupor of a creature with such high potential is suggested by the incongruous phrase, "pretty flowers under blood."

Attention is drawn to the physical danger by Willie's reaction to it:

He teaches dolls and dynamite.
Because he knows
There is a scientific thinning of our ranks.
Not merely Medgar Malcolm Martin and Black Panthers,
but Susie. Cecil Williams. Azzie Jane.
He teaches
strategy and the straight aim;
black volume;
might of mind, black flare—
volcanoing merit, black
herohood.

Here Willie refers to a concern that many blacks have that not only their leaders but their rank-and-file population is being methodically murdered. His response to the physical threat is dynamite and guns. To the spiritual threat his response is the teaching of black pride and black unity.

Blackness
is a going to essences and to unifyings

"MY NAME IS AFRIKA!"
Well, every fella's a Foreign Country.

This Foreign Country speaks to you. (*Family Pictures*, 14–15)

Africa is the inspiration in this poem as it is in many other Brooks poems, showing the importance of a sense of former glory to survival and ultimate rebirth.

V Aiming at the Rebirth of Freedom

While restraint is designed to preserve the body and the spirit of the black man and militance is an expression of and therefore sustaining evidence of the existence of the human spirit in the black man, his rebirth of freedom or a regaining of lost glory is the ultimate aim of both restraint and militance and the culminating condition of his survival. That the ultimate aim of restraint is rebirth is hinted at in some of Miss Brooks's poems that deal more directly with restraint. In "My Dreams, My Works, Must Wait till after Hell" the persona holds honey and stores bread until such time as he can "dine again." The implication is that when hell is over glory will return. In Miss Brooks's later poetry, that returning glory is alluded to in terms more definitely referring to rebirth. The same kind of hint is made in "People Protest in Sprawling Lightless Ways." People are said to "save their censures and their damns" and to pray for a "reviver," "for life again," suggesting a return to former glory. "The Sundays of Satin-Legs Smith" affords another indirect reference to rebirth. Satin-Legs is a dandy who follows a ritualistic pattern on Sundays of bathing, using his fragrant oils and lotions, dressing in his fanciest clothes, going to the movies and then to dinner with a different lady companion each Sunday, and finally taking her home to make love to her. The last six lines of the poem that refer directly to the lovemaking refer also indirectly to rebirth:

> Her body is like new brown bread
> Under the Woolworth mignonette.
> Her body is a honey bowl
> Whose waiting honey is deep and hot.
> Her body is like summer earth,
> Receptive, soft, and absolute. . . . (*World*, 31)

The images of bread and honey suggest sustenance during a period of survival as they do in "My Dreams, My Works, Must Wait till after Hell." In both poems also the anticipated foreseeable end of the present hell is alluded to. The comparison of his lady's body to "summer earth" suggests fertility and planting which in turn hint at eventual harvest and rebirth.[6]

In "In the Mecca" Alfred addresses himself to the idea of rebirth as he describes the experience of the Mecca:

> I hate it.
> Yet, murmurs Alfred—
> who is lean at the balcony, leaning—
> something, something in Mecca
> continues to call! Substanceless; yet like mountains,
> like rivers and oceans too; and like trees
> with wind whistling through them. And steadily
> an essential sanity, black and electric,
> builds to a reportage and redemption.
> A hot estrangement
> A material collapse
> that is Construction. (*World*, 402–403)

In spite of the negative reaction to the Mecca, Alfred finds some vague attraction in the Mecca which progresses toward rebirth. Described as "lean at the balcony, leaning," he is a figure of transcendence—seeing a connection between the present black experience represented by the Mecca and the survival and ultimate rebirth through collapse. "Hot estrangement" suggests an abrupt, perhaps militant, break with tradition leading to destruction and eventual "Construction" or rebirth. Rebirth is further suggested by the last sentence of "Medgar Evers":

> People said that
> he was holding clean globes in his hands.

"Clean globes," like "Construction" in Alfred's summation of his experience in the Mecca, refers to a new start—a rebirth.

Miss Brooks figuratively treats the break with tradition in "In Emmanuel's Nightmare: Another Coming of Christ." Early in the poem the abruptness of the black revolution is expressed in terms of noise and heat replacing silence, while the contrasting terms, "quiet," "sleepy," "dragged dreamily," describe the condition before the great turmoil. Miss Brooks's description of the coming of Christ is remindful of the assertion "Democracy and Christianity recommence with me" from "Riders to the Blood-Red Wrath":

> Out of that heaven a most beautiful Man
> Came down. But now is coming quite the word?
> It wasn't coming. I'd say it was—a Birth.
> The man was born out of the heaven, in truth.
> Yet no parturient creature ever knew
> That naturalness, the hurtlessness, that ease.
> How He was tall and strong!
> How He was cold-browed! How He mildly smiled!
> How the voice played on the heavy hope of the air
> And loved our hearts out! (*World*, 367)

More specifically than the general allusion in both poems to the black revolution in terms of Christian rebirth, there is a common reference to the magnanimity that results from the second coming of Christ. In "Riders to the Blood-Red Wrath" this reference is as follows:

> my Calvary
> I grind into a little light lorgnette

> Most sly: to read man's inhumanity.
> And I remark my Matter is not all.
> Man's chopped in China, in India indented.
> From Israel what's Arab is resented.
> Europe candies custody and war
>
> Behind my exposé
> I formalize my pity: "I shall cite,
> Star, and esteem all that which is of woman,
> Human and hardly human." (*SP*, 117–18)

compared with the following from "In Emanuel's Nightmare: Another Coming of Christ":

> Why, it was such a voice as gave me eyes
> To see my Fellow Man of all the world,
> There with me, listening.
>
> He had come down, He said, to clean the earth
> of dirtiness of war. (*World*, 367–69)

While both poems view the scourge of war as horrible, they both ultimately express resignation to its presence as a reality of the human condition.

The abrupt change referred to in "In Emanuel's Nightmare: Another Coming of Christ" to suggest the black revolution gives way to "of the furious Who take Today and jerk it out of joint have made new underpinnings and a Head" in "Young Africans." The directness of the reference to the black revolution and the necessary break with tradition is germane to the message of the poem. Miss Brooks suggests here the idea that black people cannot afford frivolity that is not also useful, practical, and in tune with reality. In speaking of a new utilitarian poetry she observes:

> Blacktime is time for chimeful
> poemhood
> but they decree a
> jagged chiming now.
>
> If there are flowers flowers
> must come out to the road. Rowdy!—
> knowing where wheels and people are,
> knowing where whips and screams are,
> knowing where deaths are, where the kinds kills are.

Poetry must be militant and concerned with the most vital and vulgar needs of the people. Like poetry, kindness must not be blithe but discreet, as indicated by the following passage:

> As for that other kind of kindness,
> if there is milk it must be mindful.
> The milk of human kindness must be mindful
> as wily wines.
> Must be fine fury.
> Must be mega, must be main. ·

Even kindness must be militant and guarding against seduction. The break with tradition is injurious to those who would continue to follow tradition, but the "hardheroic" are said to

> . . . await,
> Across the Changes and the spiraling dead,
> our black revival, our black vinegar,
> our hands, and our hot blood.

There is, besides the reference to black rebirth, an appeal to the black solidarity.

"Paul Robeson" continues the theme of breaking with tradition and expressing a need for unity. Maleness and adulthood, two qualities denied the black man by traditional views, are attributed to Paul Robeson, black hero:

> The major Voice.
> The adult Voice.
> Forgoing Rolling River,
> Forgoing tearful tale of bale and barge
> And other symptoms of an old despond.

"Forgoing" refers to the great personal sacrifice Robeson made in order to remain faithful to his principles. His message of black unity is suggestive of survival and rebirth:

> Warning, in music-words
> devout and large,
> that we are each other's
> harvest:
> we are each other's
> business:

> we are each other's
> magnitude and bond. (*Family Pictures*, 18–19)

The subtheme of harvest as a metaphor for rebirth is not uncommon in Miss Brooks's later poetry. "The Sermon on the Warpland" represents a continuation of the harvest subtheme, the subtheme of black unity, and that of breaking with tradition. The title itself is suggestive of the whole planting-harvest cycle. "Warpland" refers to the residual effects of the black experience which create a fertile soil for the seeds of revolution and promise a bountiful harvest of freedom. Since Miss Brooks is concerned not only with the use of Christianity as a symbol of black rebirth but also with the similar use of the concept of war, it is not far-fetched to interpret "Warpland" as also meaning "planned war." This interpretation is especially credible when the many allusions to war, strife, and holocaust that permeate the sermons on the warpland are considered.

The poem's inscription, attributed to Ron Karenga, reiterates the call to unity made in "Paul Robeson":

> "The fact that we are black
> is our ultimate reality."

The fact that black people have a common formidable goal of freedom makes it imperative that they work in unison to achieve it. The poem is an exhortation to black people to prepare to wage a bruising conflict for freedom:

> Say that our Something is doublepod contains
> seeds for the coming hell and health together.
>   Prepare to meet
> (sisters and brothers) the brash and terrible weather;
> the pains;
> the bruising: the collapse of bestials, idols.
> But then oh then!—the stuffing of the hulls!
> the seasoning of the perilously sweet!
> the health! the heralding of the clear obscure!

The double pod refers to destruction and construction together. "Collapse of bestials, idols" signifies the destruction of the traditional values while "health" is suggestive of the new order of

freedom and dignity won in a spirit of love. The fact that this
poem is a sermon and its last device is to

> Build now your Church, my brothers, sisters. Build
> never with brick nor Corten nor with granite.
> Build with lithe love. With love like lion-eyes.
> With love like morningrise.
> With love like black, our black—
> luminously indiscreet;
> complete; continuous. (*World*, 421–22)

is further evidence that in Miss Brooks's poetry the black revolution identifies figuratively with the Christian religion, particularly
the concept of spiritual rebirth.

"The Second Sermon on the Warpland" refers again both to
the struggle that the black man will encounter and to the
ubiquitous effects of the whirlwind. The black man is instructed
to live and have his "blooming in the noise of the whirlwind."
Even the fear of death and other dangers present in the struggle
must not deter the effort to live in, define, and even control the
whirlwind. The black man is being urged to wage the battle for
dignity and freedom and enjoy the fruits at the same time.

Repeated references to "time" in several of Miss Brooks's later
poems provide a clue to the meaning of the spiritual rebirth of
the black, as discussed in "The Second Sermon on the Warpland." Time is referred to in "Medgar Evers" as "The raw intoxicating time was time for better birth or final death"; in "Young
Africans" as "Black time is a time for chimeful/poemhood/but
they decree a/jagged chiming now"; and also as

> of the *furious*
> Who take Today and jerk it out of joint
> have made new underpinnings and a Head,

and in "Paul Robeson" as

> That time
> we all heard it,
> cool and clear
> cutting across the hot girt of the day. (*Family Pictures*, 18–19)

All these poems cited above deal with time in such a way as to

suggest a readiness or ripeness for harvest or rebirth. Time in
"The Second Sermon on the Warpland" is described as being
"unashamed," meaning that it is completely justified and appropriate for the black man not only to make his move toward
rebirth now but also to continue to live throughout the whirlwind. The redemptive quality of the rebirth is indicated by the
evidence of the departure from traditional values:

> A garbageman is dignified
> as any diplomat
> Big Bessie's feet hurt like nobody's business,
> but she stands—bigly—under the unruly scrutiny,
>   stands in the wild weed.
>
> In the wild weed
> she is a citizen,
> and is a moment of highest quality; admirable. (*World*, 423–26)

"The Third Sermon on the Warpland" deals more concretely
with a particular instance of rebirth. For the most part, it presents a number of different pictures of a riot in the black ghetto.
A theme expressed in the account of the riot is a complete vindication for looting, burning, and sacrificial death. The inverting
of traditional standards and values is keynoted by the inverted
interpretation of a quotation by a white philosopher which says,
"It is better to light one candle than curse the darkness." Setting
fire to buildings was their way of lighting candles in the darkness. Further evidence of the feeling of justification is the blaring
of the black philosopher:

> "I tell you, *exhaustive* black integrity
> would assure a blackless America. . . ."

Whites also ironically recognize the ripeness of the time. Whereas
the brays and screams of the black man traditionally have fallen
on deaf ears, suddenly the noise of the whirlwind has caught the
attention of the white man, who is moved to observe:

> "It's time.
> It's time to help
> These People."

The comments on the white man's observation indicate further the break with tradition:

> Lies are told and legends made.
> Phoenix rises unafraid.

As the inscription at the beginning implies, the poem captures the spirit of the black man rising renewed from the ashes of a self-consuming fire. This is the real answer to the puzzled questions of white people who ask,

> "But WHY do These People offend *themselves*?"

The sermon, then, can best be summarized in the words of the black philosopher:

> "There they came to life and exulted,
> the hurt mute.
> Then it was over.
>
> The dust, as they say, settled." (*Riot*, 16–20)

Because the aim of militance is to destroy the chains of bondage, rebirth follows militance as naturally as militance follows restraint. Though the black experience has been dotted with militant incidents, the general approach to survival has been through restraints. As militance becomes increasingly the normal approach to survival, the prospect of spiritual rebirth of the black man looms larger. Miss Brooks's poetry on black militance correspondingly almost always alludes to rebirth as a possible result.

Miss Brooks presents rebirth as a desirable probability and not as an inevitable event. In several of her poems she reminds the reader that an alternative to rebirth is death. In "Medgar Evers" she makes clear that Evers by choosing militance as an approach to survival is taking a chance that rebirth will not be the result: "The raw/intoxicated time was time for better birth or/a final death." However, although final death is mentioned, it is clear that Miss Brooks believes Evers is an agent of the spiritual rebirth of the black man. Similarly the choice of militance as an approach to survival in "Riders to the Blood-Red Wrath" is not rewarded with an unequivocal assurance of rebirth. Instead the possibility of failure (presumably final death) is presented:

I . . .

Ride into wrath, wraith and menagerie

To Fail, to flourish, to wither or to win.
We lurch, distribute, we extend, begin. (*SP*, 18)

Again, however, the tone of the poem is indication that taking the militant stance is in itself some measure a rebirth and moral victory.

A successful spiritual rebirth of blacks would affect the whites also, according to Miss Brooks. The whites would also come to embody Christian and democratic ideals and eliminate the present conditions of oppression associated with the black experience and other instances of man's inhumanity. There would be a violent reversal where the action veers to its opposite. The spiritual death would be replaced by spiritual life comprised of hope, power, glory, and dignity.

CHAPTER 7

Maud Martha

MISS Brooks is known almost entirely for her poetry. Her lone novel, *Maud Martha,* published in 1953 during the early period of her work, was not very successful. Miss Brooks says that she was too meticulous, "utilizing the possibility of every word" just as she did with her poetry and that she does not think the novel is in her "category." [1] In 1953 Miss Brooks was still forming her ideas and had not had the "great awakening" that was to come in 1967. Therefore, her novel does not include some of the themes that were popular in her poetry after 1967, such as rebirth and survival through violence.

Virtually the same poetic style, however, and use of the vignette occur in the novel as in the poetry. The same scenes and experiences inspire the same kind of characters in her poetry and prose. Each chapter presents a vignette from the life of Maud Martha. While some of the poetic themes are missing from the novel, it is somewhat more socially inspired than the early poetry but less politically inspired than her poetry after 1967.

The novel is a thinly disguised autobiographical account that depicts a black woman in a ghetto situation similar to that where Miss Brooks grew up and lived. While Miss Brooks has no sister, Helen is the embodiment of all the light-skinned or white girls with whom Maud Martha seemed to sense perpetual rivalry. The invention of Helen can be seen as a need to bring the conflict or the trouble of a quiet, unassuming, dark-skinned black woman closer with more permanence and constancy. So the fair-skinned, beautiful Helen was invented, not as a friend with whom comparisons could occasionally be made, but as a sister-foil whose daily presence was a constant reminder of the problem. Society, then, becomes parents treating their daughters differently— heightening the effect. Maud's near obsessions with color, features, and hair are paralleled in Miss Brooks's autobiography,

Report from Part One, and in her poetry.[2] There is no real plot in the novel but the order of the vignettes suggests a chronological progression from childhood, to courtship and marriage, and from marriage to motherhood. Indeed the themes that run through *Maud Martha*, in the absence of a plot, are what give the novel any cohesion. What little direction there is comes from the general movement of her thematic picture. The novel considers how Maud Martha looked at the world and how she thought the world looked at her. *Maud Martha* is a story of a woman with doubts about herself and where and how she fits into the world. Maud's concern is not so much that she is inferior but that she is perceived as being ugly.

While there are themes of death, negative displacement, survival, exaltation of the commonplace, the black-and-tan motif, and escape, they are all filtered through the point of view of an insecure, self-disparaging black woman who feels that she is homely and, therefore, uncherished because she is black and has nappy hair and "Negro features." She measures herself and her work against the standards of the world and feels that she comes out short inevitably—that white or light beauty often triumphs, though somehow unfairly—and that the depravation of the beholder is to blame. The book is also about the triumph of the lowly. She shows what they go through and exposes the shallowness of the popular, beautiful, white people with "good" hair. One way of looking at the book, then, is as a war with beauty and people's concepts of beauty. Indeed sometimes this war takes the forms of exaltation of the commonplace, escape through diversion or death, sour grapes or negative displacement, choking environment.

Although the vignettes of *Maud Martha* afford many examples of themes and subthemes, there are four main themes in the book: death, negative displacement, survival of the unheroic, and the war with beauty.

I   *Death*

The theme of death in *Maud Martha* is treated similarly to the way it is handled in Miss Brooks's poetry. In both the poetry and in the novel death is presented as an event that is part of family life. The deaths of relatives or close friends are favorite subjects and are often presented from the point of view of a child. The numerous depictions of and references to death in *Maud Martha*, as in the poetry, suggest the importance of spiritual and physical death.

Chapter 4, "Death of Grandmother," illustrates Maud's awe and esteem of death as a little girl watching her grandmother die. As in Miss Brooks's poetry (especially "Old Relative") Maud is both fearful of and fascinated with the idea of death. The harshness of the sounds and other details of the dying signifies the importance and the repulsion it has for Maud. Yet she describes her grandmother in terms of envy. Her grandmother "enjoyed" a kind of glory and importance because she was dying. The others all seem foolish compared to the grandmother; she is a queen, is exalted:

This woman, this ordinary woman who had suddenly become a queen, for whom presently the most interesting door of them all would open, who lying locked in boards with ther "hawhs," yet towered, triumphed over them, while they stood there asking the stupid questions people asked the sick, out of awe, out of half horror, half envy. (p. 13)[3]

Miss Brooks often sharply contrasts the living with the dead in order to dramatize or heighten the effect of death. In Chapter 4 she especially calls the reader's attention to this contrast by saying:

She who had taken the children of Abraham Brown to the circus, and who had bought them pink popcorn, and Peanut Crinkle candy, who had laughed—that Earnestine was dead. (p. 14)

The same technique is used in Chapter 7. Tim is presented as robust and then in juxtaposition as dead. The sharp purposeful contrast helps to heighten the sense of loss through death. In "Tim" Maud again appears to be torn between fear of and fascination with death.

Occasionally the theme of death is conveyed through an incidental reference of imagery which lets the reader know that the idea of death is prominent or perhaps latent with Maud. In Chapter 6, "Howie Joe Jones," Maud describes him as looking like an "upright corpse." His singing does not salve the eyes and sores of those who come to watch and hear him. The audience, though momentarily enlivened, returns to its grimness as it leaves the theater:

The audience has applauded. Had stamped its strange, hilarious foot. Had put its fingers in its mouth-whistled. Had sped a shininess up to its eyes. But now part of it was going home, as she was, and its face was dull again. It had not been helped. Not truly. Not well. For a hot half hour it had put that light gauze across its little miseries and monotonies, but now here they were again, ungauzed, self-assertive, cancerous as ever. The audience had gotten a fairy gold. And it was not going to spend the rest of the night, being grateful to Howie Joe Jones. No, it would not make plans to raise a hard monument to him. (p. 18)

If he is an upright corpse, "how can he imbue them with life?" [4]

Howie Joe Jones was distraction, a temporary escape from "death" but thoughts of death itself are presented as another means of escaping. The quickness with which Maud accepts the thought that she might die in "Maud Martha's Tumor" shows her ambivalent fear-fascination with death. While she seems to seize death as a way out of the grayness of her life, she is at the same time terribly frightened by death. Her contemplation of death reveals that "she was ready. Since the time had come, she was ready. . . . Her business was to descend into the deep cool, the salving dark, to be alike indifferent to the good and the not good" (p. 104). Her viewing death as a refuge bespeaks more of her view of life than of death. Like the "men of careful turns, haters of forks in the road," she is weary of having to make choices and wants to be "indifferent to the good and the not good."

Yet her joy at learning that she is not going to die demonstrates her real desire to live and love.

"You mean—I'm not going to die."
She bounced down the long flight of tin-edged stairs, was shortly claimed by the population, which seemed proud to have her back. (p. 104)

Maud's flirtation with death seems to be a silent, anomic protest against the stultifying conditions of her life.

The connection between Maud's living conditions and death are first made in Chapter 14, "Everybody Will Be Surprised." The chapter involves Maud Martha and Paul, her fiancé, planning the kinds of conditions under which they will live. Paul's dreams of having the "swanky flat" are more than offset by his firm pragmatism about living within his means. While he literally believes, for instance, that the *"Defender* will come and photograph it," he plans to consider buying "four rooms of furniture for eighty-nine dollars" and to rent a stove-heated or a basement flat because it would be cheap. Maud's reaction is first to protest and then to imagine that she sacrifices for her man. She seems to contemplate even sacrificing her life or inviting a kind of death. "She thought of herself, dying for her man. It was a beautiful thought" (p. 46).

Maud's sense of having invited a kind of death is borne out in Chapter 15, "The Kitchenette." When Maud and Paul move into the Kitchenette, Maud's enthusiasm is reflected in the use of the colors green, red, and white. After a few weeks, however, the apartment becomes a place of grayness with roaches, odors, sounds, and colors combining to "kill" her hopes and enthusiasm. The prominence of the color gray suggests death, as in Brooks's "Kitchenette Building" and other poems:

The color was gray, and the smell and sound had taken on a suggestion of the properties of color, and impressed one as gray, too. The sobbings, the frustrations, the small hates, the large and ugly hates, the little pushing-through love, the boredom, that came to her from behind those walls (some of them beaverboard) via speech and scream and sigh—all these were gray. And the smells of various types of sweat, and of bathing and bodily functions (the bathroom was always in use, someone was always in the bathroom) and of fresh or stale love-making, which rushed in thick fumes to your nostrils as you walked down the hall, or down the stairs—these were gray.
There was a whole lot of grayness here. (p. 49)

The grayness in the lives of Maud and Paul is attributable to the ennui that accompanies their powerlessness. Paul, after all, had such grandiose dreams that he is utterly distressed to find nothing of significance was happening to him or was about to happen. Paul's failure to be invited to be a member of the Foxy Cats Club in Chapter 27, "Paul in the 011 Club," is suggestive of his general failure. Maud shares his sense of failure as she observes Paul and summarized his thoughts:

The baby was getting darker all the time! She knew that he was tired of his wife, tired of his living quarters, tired of working at Sam's, tired of his two suits. (p. 105)

That the thought of even their baby is depressing rather than buoying to the couple indicates the depths of their spiritual death.

II   *Negative Displacement*

The effect of the couple's despair is intensified whenever comparisons are made between their present circumstances and past circumstances or expectations. The reader is made aware of a negative displacement through Maud Martha's sense of loss as she reflects on her condition. Paul's crudeness as described in Chapter 16, "The Young Couple at Home," increasingly disappoints her. His sleeping through a musicale, "clowning" playfully in public, not masking his need to use the bathroom, and falling asleep again leave Maud less than pleased. The titles of the books they choose to read reflect their respective tastes. Significantly he chooses *Sex in the Married Life*, which, as he nodded, "was about to slip to the floor [but] . . . she did not stretch out a hand to save it" (p. 52). The conditions of their lives had combined unhappily with their respective dreams to form a disillusionment and a self-rejection. Maud chooses *Of Human Bondage*, which suggests her feelings about her condition.

Beyond Paul's crudeness, however, the physical surrounding of the flat itself affect Maud's sense of loss. When she compares the flat with what she was accustomed to with her parents, she experiences a negative displacement. When Paul informs her that he was thinking of a stove-heated flat, she responds, "Oh, I wouldn't like that. I've always lived in steam" (p. 45). It is obvious that she considered the move a step down.

At the time of their marriage, however, she is willing to endure a temporary lowering of her condition as a "sacrifice" for her man and as testimony of her love. Later she becomes disillusioned even with love: "People have to choose something decently constant to depend on, thought Maud Martha. People must have something to lean on. But love of a single person was not enough" (p. 74).

Maud's insecurity and disillusionment are in sharp contrast to the security she felt when she was living with her parents. In Chapter 22, "Tradition and Maud Martha," she chronicles her disappointments in her marriage, lamenting the lack of wholesome traditions. She contrasts the ritual, security, and happiness of her life with her parents with the grayness, insecurity, and inconstancy of her life with Paul.

III   *Survival of the Unheroic*

Maud Martha comes to realize that even through disillusionment and spiritual death life will prevail. She notices that children in the spring are indomitable even amidst bleakness. In Chapter 2, "Spring Landscape: Details," she observes the children "mixed in the wind" as part of the bleakness but also as rays of hope. The tentative promise of the sun is like the unsure promise of the children. "Whether they would fulfill themselves was anybody's guess" (p. 7). The children are not subdued by the drab, cramped environment. Rather like Maud's commonest flower, they "come up, if necessary, among, between, or out of —beastly inconvenient! The smashed corpses lying in strict composure, in that hush infallible and sincere" (p. 127).

Maud's tendency, nevertheless, like the tendency of the mother in "The Children of the Poor," is to shield, to protect her children from the harshness of the environment. For instance, in Brooks's poem "What Shall I Give My Children? Who Are Poor," the mother laments her powerlessness:

> My hand is stuffed with mode, design, device.
> But I lack access to my proper stone.
> And plenitude of plan shall not suffice
> Nor grief nor love shall be enough alone
> To ratify my little halves who bear
> Across an autumn freezing everywhere. (*World*, 100)

The same frustration and "baffled hate" are expressed by Maud after her daughter, Paulette, has been virtually ignored by Santa Claus in a department store:

. . . Maud Martha wanted to cry.
Keep her that land of blue!
   Keep her those fairies, with witches always killed at the end, and Santa every winter's lord, kind, sheer being who never perspires, who never does or say a foolish or ineffective thing, who never looks grotesque, who never has occasion to pull the chain and flush the toilet. (p. 125)

Hidden in this plea is the need to shield the eyes of her children from the realities of life. The characters of Brooks's poetry often engage in diversions that distract them from certain unpleasant realities. Howie Joe Jones has been shown to be just this type of distraction for Maud Martha and the other patrons at the Regal. Maud Martha's infatuation with New York is a different kind of "bandage" for her eyes. She is able to "escape" to New York in her imagination.

Brooks depicts the "survival" of poor people through the everyday devices of escape and distraction. She shows Maud identifying with and taking comfort in a hardy but common flower, the dandelion. The idea that life can spring from death flourished in Brooks's poetry after 1968, but had been expressed in similar ways in *Maud Martha.*

IV   *War with Beauty*

As she identified with the dandelion in Chapter 1, "Description of Maud Martha," Maud expresses her basic need to be cherished. This chapter also lays the foundation for the struggle that occupies much of the novel. The struggle to feel cherished while knowing she was plain "was the dearest wish of Maud Martha Brown."

Immediately the comparison is made with Helen who is described as having "heart-catching" beauty. Helen symbolized the light-complexioned black woman and even white women who enjoyed favors because of their color. Maud resents this disparity of treatment and stature as vehemently as Brooks's personae in "The Ballad of Chocolate Mabbie" and "Ballad of Pearl May Lee." The issue of color and its effects occurs throughout Brooks's poetry.

Beginning in childhood with Emmanuel's harsh rejection of Maud in favor of offering Helen a ride in his wagon, the instances of the advantages enjoyed by Helen and other lighter and "more beautiful" women continue throughout the novel. Even Maud's brother, Harry, and her father favor Helen. Although Helen does nothing to deserve their loyalty as Maud does, they cherish her while paying little attention to Maud.

Each incident involving color and beauty becomes a painful memory to Maud. Her tone betrays her resentment of Helen as she reflects on the favoritism shown to Helen:

Helen was still the one they wanted in the wagon, still "the pretty one," "the dainty one." The lovely one. (p. 28)

Maud tries not to blame her family by saying she understands, but her "noble understanding" does not make the burden any lighter. Harry runs errands and opens doors for Helen but not for Maud. Their father prefers Helen's hair, worries about Helen's homework and her health, and thinks the boys dating Helen are unworthy.

In Chapter 13, "Low Yellow," the ravages of the "war" begin to show as Maud denegrates herself. Obsessed with color, features, and hair, she thinks Paul, her fiancé, would prefer a light-complexioned girl with curly hair. She imagines that Paul is self-conscious about being with her in public and that Paul wants people to know "that any day out of the week he can do better than this black gal." The passage that follows shows just how completely both Maud and Paul had ascribed to a "white" standard of beauty.

"I am not a pretty woman," said Maud Martha. "If you married a pretty woman, you could be the father of pretty children. Envied by people. The father of beautiful children."

"But I don't know," said Paul. "Because my features aren't fine. They aren't regular. They're heavy. They're real Negro features. I'm light, or at least I can claim to be a sort of low-toned yellow, and my hair has a teeny crimp. But even so I'm not handsome."

No, there would be little "beauty" getting born out of such a union. (p. 42)

In the minds of Maud and Paul, black or "Negro" features—dark skin, and nappy hair—are clearly considered ugly while beauty is associated with fine, regular features, wavy hair, and light skin. With these odds against her, Maud settles for being "sweet" instead of pretty.

Although Maud resigns herself to not being pretty, her resentment and her war with beauty continue. She repeatedly shows not only her resentment but also her envy and idolization of the white world, especially white women. Their opulence is contrasted repeatedly with the poverty and wretchedness of the blacks. This theme appears in many of Brooks's poems, such as "The Lovers of the Poor," "Beverly Hills, Chicago," and "Strong Men, Riding Horses." In Chapter 18, "We're the Only Colored

People Here," both Maud and Paul show their deference to whites as they self-consciously attend a movie downtown at the World Playhouse. The comparisons they make reveal their feelings of inferiority:

The strolling women were cleverly gowned. Some of them had flowers or flashers in their hair. They looked—cooked. Well cared for. And as though they had never seen a roach or a rat in their lives. Or gone without heat for a week. And the men had even edges. They were men, Maud Martha thought, who wouldn't stoop to fret over less than a thousand dollars. (pp. 56–57)

Maud Martha extends the comparison beyond what she sees to what she imagines and she also extends her resentment from purely physical attributes to possessions and living conditions:

But you felt good sitting there, yes, good, and as if, when you left it, you would be going home to a sweet-smelling apartment with flowers on little gleaming tables; and wonderful silver on night-blue velvet, in chests; and crackly sheets; and lace spreads on such beds as you saw at Marshall Field's. Instead of back to your kit'n't apt., with garbage of your floor's families in a big can just outside your door, and the gray sound of little gray feet scratching away from it as you drag up those flights of narrow complaining stairs. (p. 58)

Maud Martha does not like life and feels that the main reason for her deprived circumstances is her appearance. Hence her obsession with skin color, features, and hair texture. She is quite self-disparaging in Chapter 19, "If You're Light and Have Long Hair." When Maud and Paul are invited to attend the Annual Foxy Cats Dawn Ball, Maud immediately thinks that Paul does not want to go with her because of her appearance. Her insecurity is heightened when Paul dances closely with Maella, who was "red-haired and curved, and white as a white." She feels that Paul merely tolerates her and that he has to "jump over" the wall of her color in order to appreciate her inner qualities:

But it's my color that makes him mad. I try to shut my eyes to that, but it's no good. What I am inside, what is really me, he likes okay. But he keeps looking at my color, which is like a wall. He has to jump over it in order to meet and touch what I've got for him. He has to jump away up high in order to see it. He gets awful tired of all that jumping. (p. 65)

At times the frustration, whether from real or imagined causes, leads Maud to feeling like fighting, making the war open and physical. At the ball, for instance, she considers going over to Maella and scratching her upsweep down or spitting on her back or screaming. More often, however, she is content to consider herself in a psychological war with beauty or with those who are considered beautiful. Because to Maude white women fall into this category, she uses every opportunity to claim little victories at their expense. Chapter 29, "Millinery," depicts such a victory as Maud shops for a hat. Sensing the condescension of the woman manager, Maud decides to disabuse her subtly of any notions she may have that Maud could be taken lightly because she was black. She allows the manager to use all her devices and techniques in an effort to sell the hat at the listed price of $7.95. When the manager concludes that Maud would not pay more than five dollars, she offers to consult the owner. Maud coolly refutes the manager's claim that the effort to reduce the price could be made because Maud was an old customer by saying, "I've never been in the store before." Undaunted, the manager feigns a consultation with the owner and returns with the happy news that the reduction would be possible. ". . . Seeing as how you're such an old customer . . . he'll let you have it for five." Maud's relish of the triumph can be seen in the closing passages of the chapter:

"I've decided against the hat."
"What? Why, you told—But you said—"
Maud Martha went out, tenderly closed the door.
"Black—oh, black—" said the hat woman to her hats—which, on the slender stands, shone pink and blue and white and lavender, showed off their tassels, their sleek satin ribbons, their veils, their flower coquettes. (pp. 111–12)

Perhaps the ultimate encounter with a white woman occurs in Chapter 30, "At the Burns-Coopers'," when Maud hires out as a maid. The situation is very similar to that in the poem "Bronzeville Woman in a Red Hat." Driven by extreme poverty while Paul is temporarily unemployed, Maud determines to endure the condescension of Mrs. Burns-Cooper. When, however, Mrs.

Burns-Cooper and her mother-in-law reprove Maude with a stern
look because the potato parings are too thick, Maud decides
never to return to the job:

> They just looked. . . . As though she were a child, a ridiculous
> one, and one that ought to be given a little shaking, except that
> shaking was—not quite the thing, would not quite do. One held up
> one's finger (if one did anything), cocked one's head, was arch.
> (pp. 115–16)

Maud even disdains trying to explain her reasons for quitting,
although she knows Mrs. Burns-Cooper will be puzzled. She,
however, has a simple explanation for herself:

> Why, one was a human being. One wore clean nightgowns. One
> loved one's baby. One drank cocoa by the fire—or the gas range—
> come the evening, in the wintertime. (p. 116)

Maud Martha would indeed have difficulty explaining these
reasons to Mrs. Burns-Cooper. Yet these reasons underlie every
theme in the book. *Maud Martha*, in essence, depicts a sensitive
young woman grappling with the difficult problem cf reconciling
her human need to be cherished with society's aesthetic preferences and insensitivity which appear virtually to exclude her
from the ranks of the cherishable. Her recognition of her problem
and her attempts to solve it manifest themselves in the four
main themes of death, negative displacement, survival of the
unheroic, and the war with beauty.

These themes, along with the use of vignettes, a common
setting, and similar characters, appear in both *Maud Martha* and
Brooks's poetry. In the poetry the themes are emeshed in carefully drawn pictures and words while the novel is characterized
by "naked" themes for the most part. The vignettes of the novel,
while drawn from a common storehouse of experiences, appear
less "finished" than those of the poems. These differences arise
from Brooks's restriction of the novel to presenting all the
vignettes from Maud Martha's point of view, whereas she varies
the personae of the poems to fit the different situations. Ultimately, however, the themes, presented from a single point of
view, not only provide the unity within *Maud Martha* but help
to tie the novel to the larger body of Brooks's literary works.

CHAPTER 8

Black Microcosm

THE poetry and prose of Gwendolyn Brooks portray a variety of instances of human nature almost exclusively through a wide range of social aspects of the continuous black experience. The black experience itself is made up of several coherent, related phases. Individual episodes of these phases, depicted in Miss Brooks's poetry and prose as major social themes, fit logically into the total picture of both the black experience and her works. She gathers with brilliant insight a tangled snarl of the myriad events from life around her, sorts them into relevant social themes, and resynthesizes them into a meaningful whole.

Miss Brooks's poetry seems to grow as it increases in volume, not because the poet's perception becomes any more incisive, but rather because her perspective becomes more extensive. As if she were working a jigsaw puzzle, the nearer Miss Brooks comes to completing the story of the black experience the greater the accuracy with which she selects the pieces in reference to the whole picture. She has perused the story that blackness tells and she has chosen not to turn away. In her poetry her pasts, like those of Satin-Legs, lean so heavily on her that the black experience covers and colors everything she writes as if it were indeed the "little lorgnette" she mentions in "Riders to the Blood-Red Wrath." The poetry has underlying social-religious fervor which she controls "in an utter thrall." Her poetry, like the black experience, is itself a "tied storm" that she speaks of in referring to the restraint of the black man.

Miss Brooks seems to be mission-oriented with the emphasis on a serious exposé of the black man's story including his ironically heroic weaknesses that become strengths, his beguiling intuitive sense of his heritage, the obstacles he faces, and his survival. Since the poetry centers around the black man's story, which is fraught with social implications, it is inevitably largely social in nature. Because death, the fall from glory, the labyrinth, and survival, the major social themes in the poetry, correspond to the major phases of the black experience, the entire body of the poet's works can be seen as depicting an epiclike journey for the black man from a former glory through labyrinthian spiritual death to the heroic genius of survival.

Spiritual death, the first of the social themes discussed in this book, is the present general condition of blacks. Miss Brooks shows this death in many ways through references to the life around her in the black ghetto of Chicago. Her poetry reveals that the genesis of many of the dispiriting black experiences is white prejudice, manifested in a number of demeaning conditions that are depicted in Miss Brooks's poetry as curtailments of the quality and quantity of black life. Hence, there are numerous references to physical death as a prime image of the pervading spiritual death and also many references to stunted or shackled lives. For instance, the idea of canceled or deferred dreams is a manifestation of spiritual death as are depictions of feelings of inferiority and impotence; debilitating diversions such as prostitution, dandyism, and religion; resignation to death; and loneliness and despair.

All the other themes in Miss Brooks's poetry are related to death since it is the ever-present general condition from which all the other themes are either projected or recalled or particularized. The point of view or perspective begins in death and progresses toward life during the course of Miss Brooks's writing. This progression is made without any inconsistency in the subject matter. The death that the poet reveals in her early poetry is just as real in her later poems but is only infrequently featured as the central topic of a given poem. The poet's perspective in her later poems has discovered plenteous life teeming just under the veneer of death which she earlier has revealed to exist just beneath the facade of life.

The fall from glory is a use of the device of racial memory to explain death in terms that are honorable and pleasant enough to preserve the dignity and spirit of the black man. "Old Laughter" provides an example of this racial memory used to explain death. The idea that once the black man had a glorious past in a glorious land is consolation for the death he suffers. Through reference to memory, particularly of things that were better in the past, Miss Brooks evokes a sense of negative displacement.

More specifically she depicts a fall from the glorious freedom and power that the black man once enjoyed in Africa. The chapter on the fall from glory is pivotal to this book because it provides the vital link with the heights of the past which compel the directions, yearnings, and visions of the blacks. These yearnings are what compel the efforts to escape from the most pervasive element of the black people's spiritual death, the labyrinthian psychological and sociological environment which is characterized by confusion and ambivalence. The labyrinth represents the perilous, torturous route that lies between spiritual death and a reclamation of the glory of the past. Through this theme, concentrating on the psychological environment of the black man, Miss Brooks reveals the many kinds of confusion that are inherent in customs of the United States, including white confusion that stems directly from white prejudices; the thunderstruck confusion of blacks who consciously or subconsciously agree with the white prejudices; and confusions that stem from the social, political, and moral duplicity that has evolved to permeate life in the United States. Miss Brooks uses this theme also to reveal the various efforts that the black man makes to escape or solve the labyrinth, including suicide and the pursuit of other devils, gods, and formulas. The expression of this theme lends itself well to an extensive use of imagery which is sufficiently consistent in application so that it can be used as signposts that indicate the presence in a given poem of a statement on the labyrinth. Some of the numerous labyrinth images are "door," "hall," "apartment building," "street," "room," and "stairway." These and many other images from the black man's physical environment are used to evoke his mazelike psychological environment in much the same way that Miss Brooks uses physical death to suggest spiritual death.

While the fall from glory offers an explanation for death in (face-saving) honorable terms and the labyrinth describes the most pervasive feature of the black man's spiritual death, survival provides a redefinition of death. The images turn from death and confusion to "whirlwind," "blooming," "harvest," and life. The focus is not on the environment of the black man but on his inner qualities, namely his resilience and his steel. Miss Brooks applauds repeatedly the dissembling black hero who survives the general oppression. He, after all, has performed the miracle of life by being buried so that he can rise from the dead

like both Christ and the Phoenix. She also applauds the prudent
seething that is controlled in a spirit of living to fight another
day as illustrated so well by Mrs. Sallie in "In the Mecca" and
by the narrator in "Riders to the Blood-Red Wrath." She recognizes the heroic necessity for the man who has been pushed
beyond his ability to restrain himself to resort at last to militance, heedless of the personal consequences. The act of militant
heroism is necessary as a reminder that the human spirit still
lives in black men and that militance is the road that must be
taken to rebirth—perilous though it may be.

Rebirth is redemption because it involves the black man's fulfilling his concept of manhood which he has not done since before
his fall. Each black and each part of the black experience po-
tentially contains a microcosm of the complete epic movement
from former glory to surviving through spiritual death's labyrinth
to a rebirth of glory. Therefore the poet merely must select those
vignettes that best illustrate a given part of the black experience.
Miss Brooks intuitively or consciously very deftly selects and
arranges her material from the rich subject matter. As thoroughly
illustrated in her "Sermons," she relies very heavily upon harvest
and time imagery to suggest that the time is ripe for a rebirth of
freedom.

While death, survival, and the labyrinth are present realities,
both the fall from glory and the rebirth are entities that live
somewhere in the psyches of black people, through memory or
through projection into the future. The hellish present of the
blacks makes it highly desirable that they have a glorious past
and a promising future. There are beginnings that promise to
develop into rebirth of the glory that lives in the racial memories
of the black people. These memories inspire restraint and militance and point the way "back home" to rebirth of freedom that
is often symbolized by Africa. Spiritual death, then, is not a
permanent situation into which the blacks are frozen; for their
prime motivator is a sense of past glory through racial memory,
which is the seed of a hope sown in the wind to be harvested in
the whirlwind.

In the development of the social themes mentioned above,
Miss Brooks changes her perspective and her emphases as she
gains more experience as an observer and reporter. In her first
book, *A Street in Bronzeville*, Miss Brooks keynotes death images
and places very little emphasis on negative displacement and

still less on the labyrinth or survival. Also her approach is almost entirely through an exposure of situations in the black experience rather than character development. There are exceptions, of course, the most notable of which is "The Sundays of Satin-Legs Smith."

Annie Allen again largely uses the approach of exposing situations and not character development. Some highly complex social problems are discussed as illustrated by "The Children of the Poor." Various kinds of diversion,. such as high life and religion, are discussed as well. The last part of the book deals with the labyrinth as if it had just been discovered in such poems as "Truth," "One Wants a Teller in a Time Like This," "People Protest in Sprawling Lightless Ways," and "Men of Careful Turns, Haters of Forks in the Road."

The Bean Eaters, where *Annie Allen* stops, begins with poems on the labyrinth. But by the time Miss Brooks begins this book, she seems to have seen enough and synthesized enough so that she can delve deeper and with more authority into any given piece of social ground she chooses. The characters as a rule are usually more fully drawn than in the earlier poems even when the amount of space devoted to a character development is much shorter. Notable examples of clearly and concisely drawn characters are provided by "Strong Men Riding Horses" and "The Bean Eaters." Miss Brooks does not by any means, however, abandon the emphasis on situations in approaching her subject. As in the two poems cited above, the poetry is enriched by more complex themes than before, a development made possible and necessary by the mixture of efficient characterization and the presentation of a meaningful situation. While *The Bean Eaters* contains more on survival than the two previous books, it contains something on every major social theme. In fact the individual poems are generally more likely to involve several themes than are her earlier poems. For example, "The Old Marrieds" and "The Bean Eaters" both deal with old people "who have lived their day," but the latter manages to make significant statements on death, the fall from glory, and survival while "The Old Marrieds" deals mainly with negative displacement.

In *In the Mecca* the theme of death per se has definitely been relegated to a supportive position as the poems concentrate more on militance, restraint, and rebirth. The labyrinth plays a major role in "In the Mecca," although each of the other social themes is also in evidence. *Riot* and *Family Pictures* deal almost exclusively with rebirth as a result of militance, referring to death and the labyrinth only in terms of conditions that are overcome. One significant poem that does not appear in the abovementioned books is "Riders to the Blood-Red Wrath," which appears in *Selected Poems*. It deals with all of the social themes and is rather a complete summary in itself of the themes and of the poet's and the black man's changing emphases on them.

Miss Brooks's poetry is not only unified and coherent because of the inherent unity and coherence of the subject matter but also because she laces the poems together with a number of common poetic techniques that appear in identifiable patterns throughout her work. One of the techniques, for example, that Miss Brooks uses to lace the themes together is the use of oxymoron and other forms of contrasting terms to develop a theme in a given poem. She uses this technique frequently, especially to suggest the tension between the subthemes of restraint and militance as does "tied fray" in "Riders to the Blood-Red Wrath." Sometimes, however, this same technique is used to develop other ideas that reflect duplicity or paradox in the social conditions of the United States, as does "involuntary plan" in "kitchenette building." When this technique is used in widely separate poems dealing with totally different situational aspects of the black experience, it is a clue that similar themes are being treated. As a signpost that a certain theme is being handled this technique helps in the understanding of the poem being read.

Another technique is that of using her own sometimes esoteric imagery in a rather consistent manner throughout her poems so that the images themselves become signposts to indicate the interpretation of a given passage or poem. When, for instance, the term "lean" is used in "The Bean Eaters," it is a clue to look to see if there is evidence that the poet is discussing transcendence. Usually with great consistency the clue is confirmed by the context of the poem. When a variation of the same term is used in a much later poem, "Gang Girls," the connection between the ostensibly only remotely related vignettes of the two poems is made readily apparent by the common theme that runs through both of them. The use of the word "brave" to suggest "high life" or prostitution and general dissipation is another example of her esoteric but consistent imagery. It is used as early as "A Song in the Front Yard" and as late as "Do Not Be Afraid of No" to suggest high life.

Befitting the magnitude of the social messages it helps convey, Miss Brooks's tone remains serious and committed to the cause of black liberation throughout her poetry. It is best summarized by her poem "Mentors," where the speaker makes a vow to keep the dead on her mind always. That her vow is kept is indicated by the central position of death among the social themes of her poetry.

Perhaps the most important technique that Miss Brooks uses in developing her social themes is her masterful control of artful ambiguity. Demanding a great deal of creative response from the reader, her poems are all the more an embodiment of the black experience because the technique of indirection which is vital to black survival is so prevalent in them. Using the black experience and the condition of oppression at the hands of the white man as the underlying social theme of virtually all her poetry, Miss Brooks records the black man's anguish, protest, pride, and hope in his thralldom with the artful ambiguity characteristic of black United States folk poetry. The general approach of her poetry to the life around her reflects the tradition of the black spirituals, black secular slave songs, and blues ballads with their double and triple meanings that hide the underlying and sometimes subliminal meaning that was a form of unoffensive, inconspicuous, or even invisible protest.

As an extension of the intuitive beauty of ambiguity in art used to vent the pent-up feelings of a people whose survival has demanded acquiescence, Miss Brooks's poetry often couches the predominant social themes in such ostensibly displayed conventional themes as death, religion, war, sexual and Platonic love, and peace, to name a few. She also uses many commonplace concrete subjects, such as movies, pool players, old age, apartment dwellings, and physical deformity, that are so innocent or asocial in appearance that they may beguile the unperceptive reader into a superficial reading and, therefore, perhaps a superficial appreciation, missing the heart of the poetry's black message.

Miss Brooks's ability to use the tangible to explain the intangible to reveal the tangible in its proper perspective along with her continuous complexity and subtlety are assets in the overall efficacy of her poetry in conveying its social messages.

Her poetry is aligned with the black tradition of artful ambiguity and indirection and therefore communicates with a subconscious sophistication that is not possible with expression made solely on the conscious level.

While her poetry and prose are esoteric to the extent that they require a sensitivity to the black experience for maximum effect and appreciation, they are also universal to the extent that they employ ancillary messages or even pseudomessages which have universal appeal and application. The multi-leveled appeal contains elements so basic to human nature that the reader can usually draw universal meaning from the poetry and appreciate its underlying theme in proportion to his sensitivity to the black experience. As a microcosmic imitation of the black experience, Miss Brooks's works convey subliminal messages that penetrate and influence the social outlook of the reader by drawing the black experience into meaningful perspective, revealing its purposes, unity, and direction through the four major social themes of spiritual death, the fall from glory, the labyrinth, and survival.

Notes and References

Chapter One

1. *Report from Part One* (Detroit, 1972). Page references in the text identified by *R*.
2. David Littlejohn, *Black on White* (New York, 1966), p. 94.
3. "Gwendolyn Brooks: Poet of the Unheroic," *CLA Journal* 7 (December 1963): 115, 118.
4. Paul Angle, *We Asked Gwendolyn Brooks* (Chicago, n.d.), p. 4.
5. Ida Lewis, "Conversation: Gwen Brooks and Ida Lewis," *Essence*, April 1971, p. 28.
6. Arthur P. Davis, "The Black-and-Tan Motif in the Poetry of Gwendolyn Brooks," *CLA Journal* 6 (December 1962): 90–97.
7. Lewis, pp. 27–31.
8. Gwendolyn Brooks, *The World of Gwendolyn Brooks* (New York, 1971). Page references in the text identified by *World*.
9. 17 December 1949, p. 130.
10. Louis Simpson, *New York Herald Tribune Book Week*, October 1963, p. 8C.
11. Littlejohn, p. 94.
12. George Stavros, "An Interview with Gwendolyn Brooks," *Contemporary Literature* 2 (Winter 1970): 5.
13. Ibid.
14. Angle, p. 9.
15. Stavros, p. 6.
16. Ibid., p. 20.
17. Angle, p. 20.
18. Ibid.
19. *A Capsule Course in Black Poetry Writing* (Detroit, 1975), p. 4.
20. *Family Pictures* (Detroit, 1971). Page references in the text identified by *Family Pictures*.
21. Lewis, p. 31.

Chapter Two

1. Haki Madhubuti, as quoted in the Preface of *Report*, pp. 13–21.
2. Dan Jaffe, "Gwendolyn Brooks: An Appreciation from the

White Suburbs," in *The Black American Writer*, ed. C. W. E. Bigsby (Deland, Florida, 1969), II, 92.

3. Arthur P. Davis, "The Black-and-Tan Motif in the Poetry of Gwendolyn Brooks," *CLA Journal* 6 (December 1962): 91.

4. Arthur P. Davis, "Gwendolyn Brooks: A Poet of the Unheroic," *CLA Journal* 7 (December 1963): 117.

Chapter Three

1. Eugene B. Redmond, *Drumvoices* (New York, 1976), p. 272.

2. Clenora F. Hudson, "Racial Themes in the Poetry of Gwendolyn Brooks," *CLA Journal* 17 (September 1973): 18.

3. For a thorough discussion of Brooks's treatment of color preferences among black men see Arthur P. Davis, "The Black-and-Tan Motif in the Poetry of Gwendolyn Brooks," *CLA Journal* 6 (December 1962): 90–97.

4. Ibid., 92–93.

5. Hudson, p. 17.

6. Houston A. Baker, "The Achievement of Gwendolyn Brooks," *CLA Journal* 1 (1972): 24.

7. See Jaffe, p. 97.

8. Ibid., pp. 93–94.

9. Hudson, p. 19.

10. See George E. Kent, "The Poetry of Gwendolyn Brooks: Part II," *Black World*, October 1971, p. 41.

11. See Hudson, p. 17.

12. Redmond, p. 280.

13. Jaffe, p. 96.

14. Baker, pp. 25–26.

15. The ideas of death-in-life and life-in-death are treated more extensively in Part III of Chapter 5, which deals with spiritual rebirth.

16. Davis, "Black-and-Tan Motif," pp. 90–97.

17. "Poetry of the Unheroic," pp. 116–17.

Chapter Four

1. For a more detailed discussion of the black man's use of indirection see Melville J. Herskovits, *The Myth of The Negro Past* (New York, 1951), pp. 154–58. See also Albert C. Barnes, "Negro Art and America," in *The New Negro*, ed. Alain Locke (New York, 1925), pp. 19–25, for a discussion of the natural art of the black man.

2. See also Arthur Davis, "Gwendolyn Brooks: Poet of the Unheroic," *CLA Journal* 7 (December 1963): 114–15, for his comments

on the drabness of the physical environment and its effect on the unheroic inhabitants.

3. See also Arthur P. Davis, "The Black-and-Tan Motif in the Poetry of Gwendolyn Brooks," *CLA Journal* 6 (December 1962): 94–95, for comments on the imagery of this poem.

4. For other comments on the repeated last line see Davis's "Gwendolyn Brooks: Poet of the Unheroic," p. 121.

5. For a fuller explanation of Senghor's significance as prophet of negritude see Lilyan Kesteloot, "Naissance De La Negritude: 'L' Etudiant Noir,'" *Les ecrivains noirs de langue franchise* (Bruxelles, 1965), pp. 91–207.

6. The poem has more to say about survival and rebirth, each of which will be discussed in chapters dealing specifically with these themes.

7. All quotations from *Selected Poems* (New York, 1963). Page references are identified in the text by *SP*.

Chapter Five

1. See William Grier and Price M. Cobbs, *Black Rage* (New York, 1968), pp. 154–55. Thomas Jefferson, commenting on the necessity to prevent miscegenation, compared the Roman slaves with those of the United States by asserting, "Among the Romans emancipation required but one effort. The slave, when made free, might mix with, without staining the blood of his master. But with us a second is necessary, unknown to history. When freed, he is to be removed beyond the reach of mixture." The views of Jefferson, as one of the most enlightened men of the eighteenth century and as a founding father of the United States, illustrate how deeply white racism was ingrained in the fiber of the country (See Thomas Jefferson, *Notes on Virginia*, in *The Complete Jefferson*, ed. Saul K. Padover [New York, 1942], p. 665). For a more comprehensive treatment of the historical character of white racism, see Winthrop D. Jordan, *White Over Black: American Attitudes Toward the Negro, 1550–1812* (Chapel Hill, N.C., 1968).

2. Grier and Cobbs comment more fully on the sexual duplicity of whites in *Black Rage*, pp. 159–60. For an incisive discussion of the complexities and nuances of the black-white relationship, see pp. 18–31.

3. Ibid., p. 149.

4. Grier and Cobbs, in explaining what they term the *cultural paranoia* of the black man, contend, "For his own survival, then, he must develop a *cultural paranoia* in which every white man is a potential enemy unless proved otherwise and every social system is

set against him unless he personally finds out differently." For further discussion of the topic see *Black Rage*, p. 149.

5. For comments on the social and psychological effects of the white man's determination not to see certain aspects of the black man, see Grier and Cobbs, p. 23.

6. Grier and Cobbs discuss the guilt-linked *cultural paranoia* of the white man as exhibited in his fear of the black man (p. 154).

7. The perilous nature of halls and buildings as part of the labyrinth is hinted at in this pointed question from "Kitchenette Building":

> But could a dream send up through onion fumes
> Its white and violet, fight with fried potatoes
> And yesterday's garbage ripening in the hall,
> Flutter, or sing an aria down these rooms
>
> Even if we were willing to let it in,
> Had time to warm it, keep it very clean,
> Anticipate a message, let begin? (*World*, 4)

In "Mrs. Small" an association of hall and confusion is afforded by the phrase, "a—yell, a—scramble, in the hall" (*World*, 327).

8. Arthur P. Davis, expanding on the identification and significance of the setting of Miss Brooks's poetry, comments, "The scene of which Miss Brooks places her characters is always 'a street in Bronzeville,' and Bronzeville is not just Southside Chicago. It is also Harlem, South Philadelphia, and every other black ghetto in the North. Life in these various Bronzeville streets is seldom gay or happy or satisfying. The Bronzeville world is a world of run-down tenements, of funeral homes, of beauty parlors, or old roomers growning older without graciousness, of 'cool' young hoodlums headed for trouble, of young girls having abortions" ("The Black-and-Tan Motif in the Poetry of Gwendolyn Brooks," p. 91).

9. Arthur P. Davis comments on Miss Brooks's treatment of the fear of modern man, especially the black man, to make choices ("Gwendolyn Brooks: Poet of the Unheroic," p. 117).

10. Ibid., p. 118. Davis points out that the suicide threats described in Miss Brooks's poetry are indicative of the spiritual bankruptcy in the black ghetto.

11. Grier and Cobbs discuss the frustrations that black parents have providing protection and satisfactory answers to their children (pp. 51, 68).

12. Ibid., pp. 71–73.

13. Ibid., pp. 75, 149.

14. For Davis's thoughts on Miss Brooks's works as protest poetry

see "The Black-and-Tan Motif in the Poetry of Gwendolyn Brooks," p. 97.

15. Grier and Cobbs, p. 149.

16. This kind of imagery which mixes something beautiful with something repulsive is common in Miss Brooks's poetry. See "flowers upon rot" in "the funeral" (*World*, 10), "pomade atop a sewage" in "In the Mecca" (*World*, 380), and "ordure from the cream" in "Bronzeville Woman in a Red Hat" (*World*, 354).

17. George K. Kent, "The Poetry of Gwendolyn Brooks, Part II," *Black World*, October 1971, pp. 68–69.

18. Ibid., p. 68.

Chapter Six

1. Grier and Cobbs, *Black Rage*, pp. 7, 149.

2. Compare these items with an account of European goods used to trade for slaves in Africa: "Cotton textiles of all descriptions, utensils of brass, pewter, and ivory boxes of beads of many sizes and shapes, guns, and gun-powder, spirits—whiskey, brandy, and rum—and a variety of goodstuffs were some of the more important items to be exchanged for slaves" (John Hope Franklin, *From Slavery to Freedom: A History of Negro Americans*, 3rd ed. rev. [New York, 1967], p. 54).

3. Imamu Amiri Baraka, "The Legacy of Malcolm X, and the Coming of the Black Nation," *Home in New Black Voices* (New York, 1972), pp. 458–67.

4. Compare Baraka's assessment of the necessity for militance. Ibid., 462–67.

5. *Riot* (Detroit, 1969). Page references in the text identified by *Riot*.

6. The association of planting with rebirth is confirmed by the warpland sermons of Miss Brooks's later poetry.

Chapter Seven

1. George Stavros, "An Interview with Gwendolyn Brooks," *Contemporary Literature* 2 (Winter 1970): 16.

2. Ida Lewis, "Conversation: Gwen Brooks and Ida Lewis," *Essence*, April 1971, p. 28.

3. *Maud Martha* (New York, 1953). All page references in this chapter appear parenthetically in the text.

4. See Stavros, p. 15.

Selected Bibliography

PRIMARY SOURCES

1. Books

Aloneness. Detroit: Broadside Press, 1971.

Annie Allen. New York: Harper and Brothers, 1949.

The Bean Eaters. New York: Harper Row, 1960.

Beckonings. Detroit: Broadside Press, 1975.

The Black Position (A periodical). Detroit: Broadside Press, 1971.

A Broadside Treasury. Detroit: Broadside Press, 1971.

Bronzeville Boys and Girls. New York: Harper and Brothers, 1956.

A Capsule Course in Black Poetry Writing. Detroit: Broadside Press, 1975.

Family Pictures. Detroit: Broadside Press, 1971.

In the Mecca. New York: Harper Row, 1968.

Jump Bad: A New Chicago Anthology. Detroit: Broadside Press, 1971.

Maud Martha. New York: Harper and Brothers, 1953.

Report from Part One: An Autobiography. Detroit: Broadside Press, 1972.

Riot. Detroit: Broadside Press, 1969.

Selected Poems. New York: Harper Row, 1963.

A Street in Bronzeville. New York: Harper and Brothers, 1945.

The Tiger Who Wore White Gloves, or What You Really Are, You Are. Chicago: Third World Press, 1974.

The World of Gwendolyn Brooks. New York: Harper Row, 1971.

2. Articles in Periodicals

"The Assassination of John F. Kennedy." *Chicago Sun Times,* 19 December 1963.

"Boys. Black. A Preachment." *Ebony,* August 1972, p. 45.

"Children Are Writing Poetry." *Chicago Daily News,* 11 July 1964.

"A Concert of Poetry for an American Institution." *Panorama, Chicago Daily News,* 7 November 1964, p. 3.

"Dreams of a Black Christmas." *McCall's Magazine,* December 1971, pp. 136–39.

"Foreword." *New Negro Poets USA,* ed. Langston Hughes. Bloomington: Indiana University Press, 1964.

"Henry Rago." *Poetry* 115 (November 1969): 95–96.

"I Don't Like to Think of Myself as a Poet." *Panorama, Chicago Daily News*, 28 September 1963.

"In Montgomery." *Ebony*, August 1971, pp. 42–48.

"The Indivisible Man." *Book Week, Chicago Sunday Herald Tribune*, 18 April 1965, p. 2 passim.

"Introduction." *The Poetry of Black America: Anthology of the 20th Century*, ed. Arnold Adoff. New York: Harper, 1973.

"Langston Hughes." *Nation*, 3 July 1967, p. 7.

"Letter to the Editor of *Time*." *Time*, 18 October 1971, p. 6.

"Poetry with Shiver of Winter." *Chicago Sun Times*, 31 January 1965.

"Poets Who Are Negroes." *Phylon* 2 (December 1950): 312.

"Rockie Taylor Sharpens/clarifies the blur–." Preface to *Drum Song*, by Rockie Taylor (Rejumola Ologboni). Milwaukee: Ologboni, 1969.

"Thank You (A love note to all the components of *To Gwen with Love*)." *Black World*, November 1971, p. 42.

"They Call It Bronzeville." *Holiday*, October 1951, pp. 60–67 passim.

"A Time for Courage." *Chicago Sun Times*, 12 April 1964.

"The Truth and Beauty Expected from Engle." *Chicago Sun Times*, 14 March 1965.

"You Made Me and Shall Keep Me, Chicago!" *Chicago Tribune*, 6 December 1953.

3. Interviews

ANGLE, PAUL M. *We Asked Gwendolyn Brooks*. Chicago: Illinois Bell Telephone, n.d.

GARLAND, PHYL. "Gwendolyn Brooks: Poet Laureate." *Ebony*, July 1968, pp. 48–49 passim.

LEWIS, IDA. "Conversation: Gwen Brooks and Ida Lewis." *Essence*, April 1971, pp. 27–31.

STAVROS, GEORGE. "An Interview with Gwendolyn Brooks." *Contemporary Literature* 2 (Winter 1970): 1–20.

SECONDARY SOURCES

1 Books

ɔWN, PATRICIA L.; LEE, DON L.; and WARD, FRANCIS, eds. *To Gwen with Love: An Anthology Dedicated to Gwendolyn Brooks*. Chicago: Johnson Publishing, 1971. A creative tribute from writers, artists, musicians, and friends in appreciation of the poetic and civic achievements of Gwendolyn Brooks.

GRIER, WILLIAM H., and COBBS, PRICE M. *Black Rage*. New York: Bantam Books, Inc., 1968. Two psychiatrists analyze the riot conditions in late-1960s America and conclude that unabated white racism is the primary cause of this "black rage."

LITTLEJOHN, DAVID. *Black on White: A Critical Survey of Writings by American Negroes.* New York: Viking Press, 1966. Contains discussion of Gwendolyn Brooks's greatness as a poet in relation to her subject matter of the black experience.

REDMOND, EUGENE B. *Drumvoices: The Mission of Afro-American Poetry.* New York: Doubleday, 1976. Notes Brooks's Pulitzer Prize and its impact in black community; gives a brief biography; cites Brooks's "Foreword" in *New Negro Poets*, in which she speaks of the special perspective of the black poet.

2. Parts of Books

BARAKA, IMAMU AMIRI. "The Legacy of Malcolm X, and the Coming of the Black Nation," as reprinted from *Home* in *New Black Voices.* New York: New American Library, 1972, pp. 458–67. A brief history contrasting the styles and emphases of black poets between the 1930s and 1950 and recognizing the literary achievement of Gwendolyn Brooks, especially *Annie Allen* and the winning of the Pulitzer Prize for Poetry.

BONTEMPS, ARNA. "Negro Poets, Then and Now." *Black Expression.* Ed. Addison Gayle, Jr. New York: Weybright and Talley, 1969, pp. 84–85. A brief account of the poetic achievements of black poets with Gwendolyn Brooks described and receiving the most substantial critical approval of all the post-Renaissance group.

EMANUEL, JAMES E. "The Future of Negro Poetry: A Challenge for Critics." *Black Expression.* Ed. Addison Gayle, Jr. New York: Weybright and Talley, 1969, pp. 105–107. Discusses the obstacles to black poetry and cites Brooks's sonnet "First Fight. Then Fiddle" as successful poetry.

FULLER, HOYT W. "Toward a Black Aesthetic." In *The Black Aesthetic.* Ed. Addison Gayle, Jr. Garden City, N.Y.: Doubleday, 1972, pp. 3–11. Cites poet Louis Simpson's review of Gwendolyn Brooks's *Selected Poems* to illustrate how widespread white racism is in the realm of letters. (Reprinted from the *Critic.* Chicago: Thomas More Association, 1968.)

"Gwendolyn Brooks: Poet Laureate," ed. Phillip T. Drotning and Wesley W. Smith, *Up From the Ghetto.* New York: Cowles, 1970, pp. 170–76. Biographical sketch, mostly in Brooks's own words. An informative piece.

JAFFE, DAN. "Gwendolyn Brooks: An Appreciation from the White Suburbs." *The Black American Writer, Volume II: Poetry and Drama.* Ed. C. W. E. Bigsby. Deland, Fla.: Everett/Edwards, 1969. Offers a brief critical account of her major books of poetry while taking issue with the appropriateness of "black poetry" as a category for Miss Brooks's work.

RANDALL, DUDLEY. "Black Poetry." *Black Expression.* Ed. Addison Gayle, Jr. New York: Weybright and Talley, 1969, pp. 109–14.

A brief history of the movements, themes, and thought of black poetry containing comments on Gwendolyn Brooks's *In The Mecca* and the influence of militant young Chicago South Side writers.

WALKER, MARGARET. "New Poets." *Black Expression*. Ed. Addison Gayle, Jr. New York: Weybright and Talley, 1968, p. 95–97. Cites Brooks's *Annie Allen* as a racial vindication answering the charge by white critics that black poets lacked "form and intellectual acumen."

3. Periodicals

BAKER, HOUSTON A. "The Achievement of Gwendolyn Brooks." *CLA Journal* 1 (1972): 23–31. Argues that while Brooks generally employs a "white" style ("tense, complex, rhythmic verse that contains . . . me to physical complexities . . .") and a "black" content, her best work speaks a truth which transcends the barriers between the races. (Reprinted in Houston A. Baker, Jr. *Singers of Daybreak: Studies in Black American Literature*. Washington, D.C.: Howard University Press, 1974.)

BAMBARA, TONI CADE. " 'Report from Part One' " [Review]. *New York Times Book Review*, 7 January 1973, p. 1 passim. Views her autobiography as a low-keyed but beautifully moving document of the poet's growth toward self- and racial consciousness.

BENSON, BRIAN J. Review of *In the Mecca*, by Gwendolyn Brooks. *CLA Journal* 12 (December 1969): 203. Considers this collection to be strongly representative of Brooks's characteristic ability to present the emotive reactions and psychological nuances of black life.

BRADLEY, VAN ALLEN. "Negro's Life Here Effectively Portrayed in First Novel Pulitzer Poet from Bronzeville Finds Her Heroine There." *Chicago Daily News*, 30 September 1953. A brief critique of *Maud Martha*.

CALTER, BRUCE. "A Long Reach, Strong Speech." *Poetry* 103 (March 1964): 388–89. Indicates that *Selected Poems* shows Brooks to be "one of the very best poets and that her strengths are in her ability to use a really spoken language, to handle topical subject matter, and to make visible a whole and committed person behind her poems."

DANA, ROBERT PATRICK. "Double Martini and Broken Crank Shaft." *Prairie Schooner* 35 (Winter 1961–62): 357–62. Criticizes *The Bean Eaters* as being "a full cut below . . . *A Street in Bronzeville* and *Annie Allen*" because too many of the poems are characterized by "breakdowns of syntax, strained use of nouns as verbs and cliché."

DAVID, ARTHUR P. "The Black-and-Tan Motif in the Poetry of

Gwendolyn Brooks." *CLA Journal* 6 (December 1962): 90–97. Analyzes Brooks's recurrent concern with the ways that color gradations among blacks—from black to high yellow—have affected not just relationships between blacks and whites, but also those within the black community itself.

———. "Gwendolyn Brooks: Poet of the Unheroic." *CLA Journal* 7 (December 1963): 114–25. Like so many poets weaned on Eliot's *Waste Land,* Brooks finds twentieth-century men to be small in action, in imagination, and in spirit. But unlike many other poets, she tends "to appraise rather than to condemn" this unheroic pass man has to come to. She "understands and sympathizes with our littleness."

FORD, NICK AARON. "Battle of the Books: A Critical Survey of Significant Books by and about Negroes Published in 1960." *Phylon* 22 (Summer 1961): 128–29. With *The Bean Eaters,* Brooks has eliminated the pedantry and obscurity which marred *Annie Allen.* However, both emotional and intellectual involvement are often absent from these poems.

FURMAN, MARVA RILEY. "The 'Unconditioned' Poet." *CLA Journal* 17 (September 1973): 1–10. Charts Brooks's shift in three later books—*In the Mecca, Riot,* and *Family Pictures*—from an earlier "conditioned" view of American life which saw all people as basically good to an "unconditioned" view which accepts deep social division and the resultant need for blacks to assert their own, nonwhite identity.

GAYLE, ADDISON, JR. "Making Beauty from Racial Anxiety." *New York Times Book Review,* 2 January 1972, p. 4 passim. Combines personal reminiscence and criticism, concluding that *The World of Gwendolyn Brooks* "reaffirms [her] works as classics of our times." Applauds her technical achievements, but finds that sometimes her experiments render her work too obscure.

HANSELL, WILLIAM H. "Aestheticism versus Political Militancy in Gwendolyn Brooks's 'The Chicago Picasso' and 'The Wall.'" *CLA Journal* 17 (September 1973): 11–15. Two poems in *In the Mecca,* "The Chicago Picasso" and "The Wall," illustrate conclusively that Brooks had chosen to write "unequivocally" about and for black people.

———. "Gwendolyn Brooks's 'In the Mecca'" A Rebirth into Blackness." *Negro American Literature Forum* 8 (Summer 1974): 199–207. Discusses Brooks's new black awareness through a thorough explication of "In the Mecca."

———. "The Role of Violence in Recent Poems of Gwendolyn Brooks." *Studies in Black Literature* 5 (Summer 1974): 21–27. Points out that in her book *Riot* Brooks shows herself to possess now the fundamental characteristics of black militant writers:

(1) rejection of white middle-class cultural values, (2) affirmation to black selfhood, (3) destruction of anything that stands in the way of selfhood, (4) celebration of blackness.

HAZARD, E. P. "Habit of Firsts." *Saturday Review of Literature*, 20 May 1950, p. 23. Brooks discusses her attitude toward her popular acclaim and her sense of what poets have influenced her work.

HUDSON, CLENORA F. "Racial Themes in the Poetry of Gwendolyn Brooks." *CLA Journal* 17 (September 1973): 16–20. Cites the *Selected Poems* as a barometer of black attitudes toward racial issues across a thirty-year span of history and describes Brooks as particularly good at revealing the nature of racism itself, the frustrations of old people, and the "fermentation of the restless youths."

HULL, GLORIA T. "A Note on the Poetic Technique of Gwendolyn Brooks." *CLA Journal* 19 (December 1975): 280–85. Brief analysis of Brooks's style, with particular reference to her "quaint and unusual diction, imperative tone, personification, economical language, alliteration, slyly satiric humor. . . ."

KENT, GEORGE E. "The Poetry of Gwendolyn Brooks," Part I. *Black World*, October 1971, pp. 30–43 passim; Part II, *Black World*, October 1971, pp. 36–48, passim. A critical and analytical survey of Brooks's poetry showing her to be a poet of both the black experience and the human experience. The two-part essay discusses Brooks's artistic development in terms of style, themes, and perspective. The poet's own experiences are discussed as they affect her works, especially the major change in 1967.

LAING, ALEXANDER. "The Politics of Poetry." *Nation*, 7 July 1969, p. 26. States that *In the Mecca* is political in the broad, positive sense of recognizing that politics is the means of affecting or halting social change.

McCLUSKY, JOHN. "In the Mecca." *Studies in Black Literature* 4 (Autumn 1973): 25–30. Shifts in technique—clearer images, shorter and tighter lines—accompany the shift in attitude toward black consciousness. The poem is a turning point, a lead-in to the militancy of *Riot*.

MELHAM, D. H. "Gwendolyn Brooks: The Heroic Voice of Prophecy," *Studies in Black Literature* 8 (Spring 1977): 1–3. Examines stylistic elements of Brooks's poetry, particularly "In the Mecca," and asserts that there is reason to argue that she is writing of epic themes in an epiclike style.

NELSON, STARR. "Social Comment in Poetry." *Saturday Review*, 19 January 1946, p. 15. Sees *A Street in Bronzeville* as first-rate art and first-rate social document, with sympathy as its most memorable attitude. Has reservations, however, about the technical success of the sonnet sequence "Gay Chaps at the Bar."

RANDALL, DUDLEY. "On Getting a Natural" [Broadside Poster]. Detroit: Broadside Press, 1970. Poem suggests that Brooks's Afro hair style is symbolic of her physical and spiritual beauty.

REDDING, J. SAUNDERS. "Cellini-like Lyrics." *Saturday Review*, 17 September 1949, p. 23 passim. Considers *Annie Allen* to be "as artistically sure, as emotionally firm, and as esthetically complete as a silver figure by Cellini," but expresses fear that her work may be turning to a too-narrow audience (of blacks).

"Review of *Annie Allen*, by Gwendolyn Brooks." *New Yorker*, 17 December 1949, p. 130. Notes that these poems show a remarkable sense of form and also much experimentation, but not all of the latter is successful.

"Review of *Annie Allen*, by Gwendolyn Brooks." *United States Quarterly Book List*, March 1950, p. 20. Points out that Brooks has shifted from realism to lyric emotion, and also to elaborations and experimentation in language. The latter sometimes fail, but her abiding and natural sense of form hold the book together.

"Review of *A Street in Bronzeville*, by Gwendolyn Brooks." *New Yorker*, 22 September 1945, p. 88. Considers the work a successful crossing of folk poetry and traditional poetic forms with sincerity and lack of sentimentality keynoting the tone of the work.

"Review of *In the Mecca*, by Gwendolyn Brooks." *Virginia Quarterly Review* 45 (Winter 1969): xx. Cites a new manner and a new voice for Miss Brooks that is better than her earlier work in its honesty, poorer in its loss of music and control.

"Review of *Maud Martha*, by Gwendolyn Brooks." *New Yorker*, 10 October 1953, p. 153. Indicates the book is less a novel than a series of sketches and that its style is "not quite sharp or firm enough" to do justice to the abilities Brooks has shown in poetry.

ROSENTHAL, M. L. "In the Mecca." *New York Times Book Review*, 2 March 1969, p. 14. Considers the long title poem to be the best in the collection, containing moments of great power and horror; but it is too baroque, too embellished with "alliteration, internal rhymes, whimsical and arch observations—that distract from its horror almost as if to conceal the wound at its center."

SHANDS, ANNETTE OLIVER. "Gwendolyn Brooks as Novelist." *Black World*, June 1973, pp. 22–30. Discusses strengths and weakness of Brooks's *Maud Martha*.

SIMS, BARBARA B. "Brooks's 'We Real Cool.'" *Explicator* 58 (April 1976). Explores the implications behind the brief, telegraphic lines, with particular concern for the sharp ironic twist of the last line in the poem.

TOWNS, SANDAR. "Beckonings." *Black World*, December 1975, pp. 51–52, 87–88. Describes the movement of Brooks's poetry from elitist before 1967 to black nationalistic between 1968 and 1975 to questioning and disillusioned since 1975. *Beckonings* continues the nationalist movement but tempers the need for order and beauty with awareness of the chaos and strife in the black experience.

WEBSTER, HARVEY CURTIS. "Pity the Giants." *Nation*, 1 September 1962, pp. 96–97. Reviewing *A Street in Bronzeville, Annie Allen,* and *The Bean Eaters,* Webster finds that Brooks has grown steadily in her accomplishments and that her best poems are usually those least overtly concerned with racial issues.

WILDER, AMOS N. "Sketches from Life." *Poetry* 67 (December 1945): 164–66. Finds much of the subject matter in *A Street in Bronzeville* to be "sure-fire on easy-mark situations," but respects her close observations of life's details and her sophistication of craft and education.

4.   Unpublished Study

CLYDE, GLENDA ESTELLE. "An Oral Interpreter's Approach to the Poetry of Gwendolyn Brooks." Diss. Southern Illinois University, 1966. Analyzing the poetry linguistically, this study finds Brooks's strengths to lie in "pungent images' staccato and syncopated rhythmic effects created by abrupt and partial statements, intermingled long and short lines, and line endings; and fully developed, involved individuals for speakers."

Index